HOW TO RAISE A MODERN-DAY JOSEPH

HOW TO RAISE A MODERN-DAY JOSEPH

A PRACTICAL GUIDE FOR GROWING GREAT KIDS

An Awana Resource

LINDA MASSEY WEDDLE

David C Cook
transforming lives together

HOW TO RAISE A MODERN-DAY JOSEPH
Published by David C. Cook
4050 Lee Vance View
Colorado Springs, CO 80918 U.S.A.

David C. Cook Distribution Canada
55 Woodslee Avenue, Paris, Ontario, Canada N3L 3E5

David C. Cook U.K., Kingsway Communications
Eastbourne, East Sussex BN23 6NT, England

David C. Cook and the graphic circle C logo
are registered trademarks of Cook Communications Ministries.

The Web site addresses recommended throughout this book are offered as a resource to you. These Web sites are not intended in any way to be or imply an endorsement on the part of David C. Cook, nor do we vouch for their content.

Unless otherwise noted, all Scripture quotations are taken from the *Holy Bible, New International Version*. *NIV*. Copyright © 1973, 1978, 1984 by International Bible Society. Used by permission of Zondervan. All rights reserved. Scripture quotations marked NKJV are taken from the New King James Version. Copyright © 1982 by Thomas Nelson, Inc. Used by permission. All rights reserved.

ISBN 978-1-4347-6531-4
eISBN 978-1-4347-0027-8

© 2009 Awana® Clubs International

The Team: Terry Behimer, Thomas Womack, Sarah Schultz, Jack Campbell, and Karen Athen
Cover Design: Amy Kiechlin
Cover Image: Getty Images, The Image Bank, John Coletti

Printed in the United States of America
First Edition 2009

2 3 4 5 6 7 8 9 10

071409

Contents

INTRODUCTION

A JOURNEY WORTH PLANNING

For parents like you … in churches like yours … this book is a practical guide for a child's spiritual development—a journey in which parents *and* churches work *together* to raise kids who know, love, and serve the Lord.

Much of the vision and purpose for such a journey is discussed in my friend Larry Fowler's book *Raising a Modern-Day Joseph.* The book you hold in your hands—*How to Raise a Modern-Day Joseph*—focuses more on the *practical* side of that. It gives parents a workable plan for putting this vision and purpose to work in their everyday family life.

NO GUARANTEES?

Like Larry's book, this one is needed because we're in the midst of a crisis. The statistics stagger us as we read about, hear about, and see young people walking away from their faith.

We are surprised that this could be happening, since after all …

- our churches provide nurseries, Sunday school, vacation Bible school, Awana, youth ministries, and every other kind of kid and youth program imaginable.
- our children's ministry curriculum is more entertaining, colorful, and professional looking than ever before.

- the market is flooded with "Christian" action figures, mugs, pencils, wallpaper, wallets, posters, linens, T-shirts, and toys, many decorated with clever "Christian" sayings.
- radio stations play Christian music twenty-four hours a day, and television channels broadcast a never-ending selection of messages from both local churches and polished, smooth-talking televangelists.

And here's an even tougher dilemma: Why does a kid from one home walk away from the Lord, while a kid in another home stays true to Him—yet the families in both homes have attended the same church, Sunday school, vacation Bible school, Awana program, etc.?

What happened? What's the difference?

Before going further, I need to say this:

No plan,

no curriculum,

no humanly written book,

no pastor,

no teacher,

no parent …

can absolutely *guarantee* that a young person will *not* walk away from what he or she has been taught.

God works with His people individually, and each individual must make the choice to trust Christ as Savior. Each one chooses to walk with the Lord or to walk away from Him. After all, even with the first two kids we read about in the Bible, one had a criminal record.

The absence of such a guarantee is due to sin.

Scripture declares that the whole world is a prisoner of sin, so that what was promised, being given through faith in Jesus Christ, might be given to those who believe. (Galatians 3:22)

So yes, unfortunately, children don't come with guarantees.

But God's Word *does* come with a guarantee: If we trust the Lord Jesus Christ as Savior, believing that He died and rose again, we're promised …

- the forgiveness of sin (bridging the separation between imperfect people and a perfect God).
- eternal life.
- a future in an unimaginably perfect heaven.

That's some guarantee!

No, we as parents don't have guarantees, but we do know that children who grow up in strong, Christ-centered homes—where God's Word is both taught *and* lived—are more likely to live godly lives as adults. But let's take a glimpse at what is typically going on in many families.

A CHURCH AND PASTOR PROBLEM?

I grew up as a preacher's kid and, as an adult, became a preacher's wife—I know firsthand how often the preacher and the church get blamed for parental failures.

I remember one Sunday morning after the church service when my husband was shaking hands with people filing out of the auditorium. Suddenly a visibly upset mother stormed into the lobby, yelling. She said her son had been knocked over by other boys in the parking lot.

My husband's first reaction was to call an ambulance, but the mom said that wasn't necessary; her son just scraped his knee. "But," she shouted, pointing to my husband, "this is *your* fault."

"Why?" he asked. He could see our own two kids talking with friends nearby, so they weren't the ones who had knocked down the woman's son. So why was the incident his fault?

"Because it's *your* church," the woman screamed. (Well, that wasn't true; the church belongs to the people as much as to the pastor.) "And so they're *your* responsibility."

However, that true story is a picture of what many people do spiritually.

Just as many parents leave the physical well-being of their children up to the church (the drop-them-off-in-the-parking-lot syndrome), so many parents do the same with their children's spiritual well-being, training, and guidance: They drop them off in the parking lot and let the church do the nurturing (whether or not the parents are even in the same building).

Maybe you feel this way too—at least to some extent. After all, you make sure your children go to church for every kids' activity possible, so you figure the church's pastors, teachers, and leaders are covering that spiritual-training part of your kids' lives. You're busy doing other things, like working long hours to provide for your family, which *is* your responsibility.

Deep inside, you hope those people at the church are doing it right. And if your kids walk away from the Lord someday, you'll certainly have something to say about the church's failure, since spiritually raising your kids is its job.

Right?

Well … no!

FROM THE START

Let's review some essentials of what the Bible says about the family.

The Family Is the First Group God Created

The family unit came before towns or countries and before churches, youth programs, basketball teams, or Facebook. God immediately created the marriage partnership; in fact, by the second chapter of Genesis, God had already established marriage:

> For Adam no suitable helper was found. So the LORD God caused the man to fall into a deep sleep; and while he was sleeping, he took one of the man's ribs and closed up the place with flesh. Then the LORD God made a woman from the rib he had taken out of the man, and he brought her to the man. (Genesis 2:20–22)

And already by the fourth chapter in Genesis, we learn about children.

The Family (Marriage Partnership) Is a Picture of Christ and the Church

Paul says it this way:

Submit to one another out of reverence for Christ. Wives, submit to your husbands as to the Lord. For the husband is the head of the wife as Christ is the head of the church, his body, of which he is the Savior. Now as the church submits to Christ, so also wives should submit to their husbands in everything. Husbands, love your wives, just as Christ loved the church and gave himself up for her to make her holy, cleansing her by the washing with water through the word, and to present her to himself as a radiant church, without stain or wrinkle or any other blemish, but holy and blameless. (Ephesians 5:21–27)

Family "Rules" Are Listed Throughout the Bible

Here's an example:

Wives, submit to your husbands, as is fitting in the Lord. Husbands, love your wives and do not be harsh with them. Children, obey your parents in everything, for this pleases the Lord. Fathers, do not embitter your children, or they will become discouraged. (Colossians 3:18–21)

Family Members Need to Encourage Each Other

Paul pointed to family encouragement as a model for the entire church:

We were gentle among you, like a mother caring for her little children.… For you know that we dealt with each of you as a father deals with his own children, encouraging, comforting and urging you to live lives worthy of God, who calls you into his kingdom and glory. (1 Thessalonians 2:7, 11–12)

The family has the *primary* responsibility in the spiritual training of children. But families also need the church to come alongside them to nurture their kids, to provide Christian friendships from like-minded families, and to give complementary spiritual training. (We'll look at all that more closely later.)

SOMEONE WHO KNEW, LOVED, AND SERVED GOD

The goal of Awana (the ministry I serve with) is to train children and youth to grow into adults who *know, love, and serve the Lord.* We've come to see that this is also a priority goal for parents in training their children.

And as a biblical example of a young person who grew up to know, love, and serve the Lord, it's hard to find a better example than Joseph in the Old Testament—not that he came from a perfect family.

Most children know about Joseph. They know he received a unique coat from his father—and our perception of that is a knee-length coat with rainbow-colored stripes. But why would grown men (his older half-brothers—see Genesis 30:1–25) care about their little brother's multicolored coat? The Hebrew word here for "coat" refers to a full-length tunic—sleeves to the wrist, the hem to the ankles. This was the style of coat worn by rich young men. They didn't have to work (they had slaves or servants to do that), and they had a position of honor both in the home and in the community.

Joseph's full-length coat was probably made of white linen, with bands of colorful embroidery as trim. By contrast, working men wore plain, looser-fitting, shorter garments so they could climb over rocks and take care of their sheep—they needed to move quickly and not be hindered by long clothing. So the brothers weren't jealous of the colors of Joseph's coat but rather the implied position Joseph held in wearing such a garment.

Joseph lived in Hebron. The word *Hebron* means "community" or "fellowship." Joseph had fellowship with his father, but this wasn't a family that had a lot of fellowship with one another. I don't think dinnertime conversations were leisurely discussions about the price of sheep feed or the Hebron weather.

The truth is, Joseph came from a dysfunctional family. This is obvious when you read in Genesis 30 about the intrigue involving his mother, his mother's sister, their servants, and drugs (mandrakes, which were seen as narcotics or aphrodisiacs). Rachel and Leah were both jealous women who were willing to have their servants lie with Jacob so they could win the who-can-have-the-most-sons race. And when

Reuben brought home some mandrakes, Rachel desired them so much she was willing to "sell" Leah a night with Jacob to get her hands on them.

This of course isn't part of the biography we read about in Sunday school, but these events are worth noting here. Out of this mess, the Lord brought Joseph, a young man who never wavered from the assurance that God was with him; a young man with a true heart desire to know, love, and serve the Lord.

We know that Joseph's brothers sold him into slavery and that he ended up in Egypt. We know he quickly gained power and influence in Potiphar's house, then quickly lost it when fleeing the temptations of Mrs. Potiphar. Yet even when put in prison, Joseph knew that God was with him, and he remained faithful. Later, because he interpreted the king's dream, he was made a VIP and placed in charge of the entire land of Egypt. In that position, he was able years later to publicly forgive his brothers.

Through it all, Joseph concluded that it wasn't his brothers who sent him to Egypt, but *God.* God had a plan for him, and Joseph listened to God and fulfilled His plan—something he was later able to testify about to his brothers: "God sent me ahead of you to preserve for you a remnant on earth and to save your lives by a great deliverance" (Genesis 45:7).

Joseph's life in particular reflected five godly character qualities—we'll call them "Master Life Threads," as Larry Fowler does in *Raising a Modern-Day Joseph*—that were woven into the very being of who he was and how he lived his life:

- *Respect* for the awesomeness and authority of God (Genesis 39:6–9)
- *Wisdom* for living life based on a knowledge of God (40:6–8)
- *Grace* in relationships with others (41:51–52)
- A sense of *destiny* and purpose that came from God (45:4–10)
- A *perspective* for life based on the sovereignty of God (50:15–21)

These Master Life Threads are also desired characteristics in the lives of our own children—as they learn to *know, love,* and *serve* the Lord.

We know that Joseph *knew* about the Lord. God was the God of his father, Jacob. As Joseph's life continued in surprising new situations—as head of Potiphar's household, as a prisoner, and finally as the man in charge of all of Egypt—he continued following the Lord. Over and over in the biblical account of Joseph's life, we read that the Lord was *with* him, as in Genesis 39:21: "The LORD was with him; he showed him kindness and granted him favor in the eyes of the prison warden."

We know that Joseph *loved* the Lord because of the way he lived his life, refusing to be drawn into the temptations of a rich and powerful household, and because of his exemplary forgiveness toward the brothers who had wronged him: "But Joseph said to them, 'Don't be afraid. Am I in the place of God? You intended to harm me, but God intended it for good to accomplish what is now being done, the saving of many lives. So then, don't be afraid. I will provide for you and your children.' And he reassured them and spoke kindly to them" (Genesis 50:19–21).

And we know that Joseph *served* the Lord—by making righteous choices, by administrating the seven years of plenty, and by giving food not only to the people of Egypt but to those from other countries as well. As the famine intensified and "the people cried to Pharaoh for food," Pharaoh responded, "Go to Joseph and do what he tells you" (Genesis 41:55).

MODERN-DAY JOSEPHS

What Christian parents wouldn't want their child to grow up to be a modern-day Joseph—a young person who reflects those five Master Life Threads and who knows, loves, and serves the Lord?

For many parents (and maybe this includes you), their children are already becoming Josephs. They do excellent jobs spiritually nurturing their children. They daily teach their kids God's Word by guiding them toward recognizing the need to trust Christ, praying with them, reading the Bible together, encouraging Scripture memorization, explaining difficult words and concepts, and talking about the qualities of the Christian walk. Then they live out God's Word in everyday life. They take their responsibility seriously.

Then there are other parents who simply don't think about their children's spiritual training. These parents flounder through life, not learning much themselves about what the Bible actually says, and they couldn't begin to explain the difference between Genesis and Galatians. Yet they're law-abiding citizens and church-attending Christians. They figure their kids will turn out okay. After all, they get their kids to Sunday school and even sent them once to a Christian summer camp.

But the majority of Christian parents are somewhere in the middle. They desire to be spiritual nurturers of their children, but *they don't know how.* They might be intimidated that they won't choose the right words. (What if my child asks me to explain eschatology or something?) Or they don't know where to find a plan that shows them how to be a spiritual nurturer. (They may not even realize they should *have* a plan.)

Furthermore, you probably know some adults who grew up without any spiritual nurturing in the home, yet who are now pastors, missionaries, church leaders, or shining witnesses in the secular workplace. The Lord used someone besides a parent to mentor that child or gave the child a desire for Bible study that transformed her into someone who truly wants to know, love, and serve the Lord.

GOAL AND PLAN

If our destination is having a child who develops Joseph-like characteristics—knowing, loving, and serving the Lord—what's the itinerary or plan for that journey?

The lack of such a plan often becomes *the* roadblock in our children's spiritual development—and getting past that roadblock is what this book is all about. This book is not a step-by-step itinerary but more of an atlas where you pick and choose which stops to make in your own family journey—because we know all families are different, with different schedules, different interests, and different personalities.

Our desire is to give your family (and your church) ideas—*lots* of ideas—for helping to spiritually nurture your children. But as the parent, *you* need to devise the route.

It's a plan that involves *both* parents—and the church as well.

Dad

The father is the head of the house and the God-ordained leader of the home. Dads and moms need to work together to spiritually raise their children.

A spiritually strong dad will …

- pray with his children.
- lead the children in Bible study and worship.
- take an interest in what the child is learning at church.

- teach his children Bible verses, Bible concepts, and Bible truths.
- discuss challenging questions, cultural events, and concepts with his children.
- model a Christlike attitude in his daily life.

Unfortunately in too many homes, Mom is by herself in doing all of this. Dad might drive the family to church, but he doesn't take any real responsibility in the child's spiritual development.

If you're a father, know this: God has given you a job to do. Your responsibility is to do it. You can't expect your child to grow into a God-honoring adult when he sees you ignore the Bible, find every excuse possible to avoid church, and live a life that's inconsistent with what God says in His Word.

Mom

Children need *both* parents involved in their spiritual training, and that's the basic scenario presented throughout this book. It's a sad situation when Dad is faithfully living for the Lord, but Mom doesn't want any part of it.

Mom needs to be an active part of the praying, teaching, discussing, and modeling too. For example, sometimes Mom's the one who spends a half hour before or after school helping her children work on a memory verse, and when Dad gets home, he can enthusiastically listen to the children recite the verse. This is a joint effort. Both parents are huge influencers.

You might be a single mom and already feel defeated because you don't have a husband to help you out. You can still teach your children from God's Word and live an exemplary life. In your situation, the partnership of the church may be more important than usual. Hopefully your church has good male role models teaching younger children, so your children can profit from a masculine influence.

A good example of one parent spiritually training a child is that of Eunice and her son Timothy (2 Timothy 1:4–5). Eunice did have the help of her own mother, Timothy's grandmother, but she didn't have any help from her unbelieving Gentile husband. Timothy's mom and grandma taught him the Old Testament Scriptures and exemplified godly lives. When the apostle Paul came along and taught Timothy about the Son of God and His sacrifice on the cross, Timothy was ready to trust Christ as Savior. Timothy became Paul's son in the faith (1 Timothy 1:2), and Paul recognized the foundation that Timothy's mom and grandma had laid.

Many single parents do great jobs in spiritually training their children. If you're a single parent, or your spouse isn't interested in God and His Word, you need to surround yourself with adults who can give you and your children support and encouragement.

Fitting into Your Schedule

When, where, and how do we spend time spiritually training our children?

The following verses from Deuteronomy give clear instruction that we should look for teaching opportunities to spiritually train our children every moment of our lives.

> Fix these words of mine in your hearts and minds; tie them as symbols on your hands and bind them on your foreheads. Teach them to your children, talking about them when you sit at home and when you walk along the road, when you lie down and when you get up. Write them on the doorframes of your houses and on your gates, so that your days and the days of your children may be many in the land that the LORD swore to give your forefathers, as many as the days that the heavens are above the earth. (Deuteronomy 11:18–21)

In a real sense, spiritual training in the home is ongoing and never ending. It's really a part of everything you do.

But we also need to set aside specific times when we come together as a family to pray to, honor, and worship the Lord and to study and memorize His Word. Some families enjoy singing or playing instruments together. Others read a page from a devotional book.

One teenager said, "Our family wasn't musical, so that wasn't part of our activities. But we did other things, such as making rebuses of Bible verses."

You might set aside a time each day for spiritual focus—at the breakfast or supper table or before bed. Or you could plan family nights when an entire evening is dedicated to a lesson, an activity, and a special treat. (Be careful you don't present the activity as more important and fun than the lesson. Bible study can and should be a great experience.)

Maybe your family's schedule is so complicated that you can't have a regular set time for spiritual focus, but you can still conscientiously meet together as opportunities present themselves to pray to, worship, and learn about the Lord.

A couple of considerations in all this:

- Sometimes families are diligent in having family devotions, but that's the only time their children hear about the Lord. Because Dad prays and reads a page from a devotional book, he feels he's taken care of his spiritual-leadership responsibilities. Five minutes later, the children hear him swear when opening the gas bill or see him confront a neighbor because the neighbor's dog messed up the lawn. What he verbally taught is negated by the way he lives his life.
- Families are different. One guy diligently teaches his kids from the Bible, helps them with their memory verses, and consistently lives a godly life, yet he feels guilty. He knows of another family that spends thirty minutes of concentrated training at the supper table each night, but his irregular work schedule doesn't allow him to do that. He is, however, doing a great job. We need to focus on our own families, not on what someone else is doing.

We as parents need to work together to develop the itinerary for our own families, keeping our eyes on the goal of raising children who know, love, and serve the Lord.

Your Church

Whether large or small, your church is your best partner in raising your children.

In fact, the size of the church doesn't really matter. Megachurches have the money and staff to provide exciting programs for both parents and children, and those programs can be good. But smaller churches can be better at giving a child a sense of security, family, and nurturing that you don't always find in larger churches.

So church size isn't important. What *is* important is the *attitude* of the church and the pastor toward kids. Does your church leadership really care about kids? Do they see the value in children's ministry and provide the necessary resources to spiritually disciple children? Do they occasionally visit children's or youth ministry programs to give the lesson, answer questions, or simply greet the participants? Do they make an effort to learn the names of the kids, or do they know your three teenagers (who have been attending the church since birth) only as the Hansen kids?

If your church doesn't see the importance of encouraging families, maybe *you* could be the catalyst to begin the initiative.

After this book's part 1 (which focuses on giving *parents* specific age-appropriate suggestions for their child's spiritual development), part 2 will focus especially on practical ways *the church* can partner with you in this task. Be sure to explore what's presented in part 2, and become familiar with ideas of how churches and families can work together.

PLANNING YOUR FAMILY'S SPIRITUAL JOURNEY

The ideas in this book are suggestions. No parent can do everything, just as no church can do everything. Our goal is to give you plenty of ideas to help get you started and keep you going. ⸙

So let me lay out what you'll find in each chapter in part 1, which is especially geared for you as a parent.

Life Threads

Each chapter targets a different stage of a child's life and will focus on an appropriate life thread (reflecting a quality that Joseph displayed in his life).

Here are these life threads for each age category:

Preschoolers (ages 2–5)	*Respect*
Early Elementary (ages 5–8: kindergarten through second grade)	*Wisdom*
Older Elementary (ages 8–11: third through sixth grades)	*Grace*
Middle School (ages 11–14: seventh and eighth grades)	*Destiny*
High School (ages 14–18: ninth through twelfth grades)	*Perspective*

At the beginning of each chapter, you'll find listed again the life thread to focus on for that stage in your child's life.

By the way, if you're looking at this list and thinking, *Great, but my child is already twelve years old!*—that's okay. Yes, you've missed some prime training opportunities, but you can catch up. Review the sections for preschoolers and elementary-age children, and teach the principles to your child using explanations and activities appropriate for a twelve-year-old. Instead of regretting what you missed, focus on the present and look to the future. These concepts are good for all ages— including adults.

What They're Like

Early in each chapter, the What They're Like section lists ten characteristics about that particular age category. Understanding these characteristics will give you a great head start in helping your child grow spiritually.

What They're Asking

The What They're Asking section in each chapter lists the kinds of questions that kids in this age-group typically ask about God and the Bible. You'll also find suggested answers to a few of the questions.

These questions came from a "Biggest Question Survey" sponsored by Awana. A few years back, we asked four thousand children and teenagers, "What's your biggest question about God and the Bible?" These children and teenagers all had some Bible background (though, after looking at their questions, we surmised that some didn't remember much of it). Then we determined the most-asked questions for each age-group.

But don't stop with reading what other kids have asked; ask your own children for their biggest questions about God and the Bible.

What You Can Do

In the What You Can Do section of each chapter, you'll find a wealth of practical suggestions for what you as a parent can do to help your child's spiritual growth in each stage. This begins with a short section about helping your child make the all-important decision to trust Christ as Savior.

Bios and Verses

Here you'll find appropriate Bible biographies and Scripture memory verses to explore and learn with your children.

(At Awana, we substitute the word *biography* for *story* to emphasize that what comes from the Bible is true and not fictional. We explain that a biography is a true story about someone.)

What Not to Do

Sometimes we hinder more than we help. Each chapter includes a What Not to Do section, where you'll find common errors to avoid in each stage of your child's life.

Checklist

Each chapter also includes a checklist of basic attainments to look for in your child's spiritual development.

Family Itinerary

Finally, the Family Itinerary section in each chapter is a worksheet to help you develop your plan and goals for your child's spiritual journey in each stage.

Here are a couple of samples of completed itineraries from two families, one with younger children and one with teenagers:

A SAMPLE ITINERARY FOR A FAMILY WITH YOUNG CHILDREN

Our spiritual goals for the year are:

1. *Teach Emma and Jacob that God created the world.*

2. *Teach Emma and Jacob that God loves each one of us.*

3. *Teach Emma and Jacob that the Bible is God's book.*

4. *Teach Emma and Jacob that Jesus is God's Son.*

5. *Teach Emma and Jacob that we're to obey God.*

Our family verse for this year is:

Genesis 1:1

We'll also study the following six additional verses (one every two months) about God and His character:

1. *Psalm 23:1*

2. *Psalm 33:4*

3. *Psalm 147:5*

4. *Matthew 28:20*

5. *Romans 6:23*

6. *1 John 4:10*

We'll also study the following six Bible biographies (one every two months):

1. *Adam*

2. *Joseph*

3. *Heman*

4. *Josiah*

5. *David*

6. *Christ's birth*

We'll also do a more extensive study on this person in the Bible:

Heman in 1 Chronicles 25:5–7. We'll learn how he and his family sang in the temple. We'll learn a song together and sing at church.

Here are other activities our family will do together to learn about Bible characters:

1. *We'll watch a series of DVDs on Bible characters (a set we were given that's factual).*

2. *We'll visit Grandpa and Grandma and look at the pictures they took in Israel.*

3. *We'll study Josiah and other Bible characters who served God even though they were young.*

4. *We'll do several crafts using natural materials from the outdoors as we talk about God's creation. These will include leaf tracings, pictures on sun-sensitive paper, and drying flowers.*

5. *We'll teach Emma and Jacob to identify five birds and five flowers, explaining that they were all created by God.*

Here are some themes for family fun nights we would like to do this year:

1. *We'll build a birdhouse together and learn about ten birds in our area of the country, and we'll thank God for creating a wonderful variety of birds.*

2. *We'll make a mural of David watching his sheep for the basement wall.*

3. *We'll invite Grandpa and Grandma to family night so they can hear Jacob and Emma say their verses.*

4. *We'll make a book of all the different Bible biographies Jacob and Emma have learned at church this year.*

5. *We'll visit the zoo.*

6. *We'll make cookies for the woman down the street who's homebound.*

Our family has completed this year's family itinerary and met our spiritual goals.

   (Signed by each family member)

A SAMPLE ITINERARY FOR A FAMILY WITH CHILDREN IN HIGH SCHOOL

Our spiritual goals for the year are:

1. *Study the book of Ephesians together.*

2. *Encourage Andrew and Amanda to teach and mentor younger children, whether that's younger cousins or at church.*

3. *Discuss a biblical worldview and what that means as Andrew and Amanda head off to college.*

4. *Have open, honest discussions about difficult cultural issues.*

5. *Encourage Andrew and Amanda to write down any questions they may have about God and the Bible and to work through those questions as a family.*

6. *For Andrew and Amanda to serve by singing and playing guitar at the rescue mission once a month.*

Our family verse for this year is:

Joshua 24:15

This year we'll do the following family research project:

We'll focus on creation. The project will culminate with a week at creation camp this summer.

We'll memorize this chapter from the Bible:

Ephesians 2

We'll read (either as a family or individually) the following books:

1. Evidence That Demands a Verdict *by Josh McDowell*

2. Mere Christianity *by C. S. Lewis*

Our family service project this year will be:

Serving at the soup kitchen on Thanksgiving and Christmas

Our family has completed this year's family itinerary and met our spiritual goals.

(Signed by each family member)

PART ONE
(ESPECIALLY FOR PARENTS)

CHAPTER 1

AT THE STARTING LINE
(AGES 0–2)

This chapter won't have all the various components you'll find later for the older age-groups, but it's important to realize how much parents of infants can do in launching the spiritual training of their children.

In fact, this spiritual training actually begins *before* your child is born.

BEFORE THE BIRTH

I remember the day I found out I was pregnant. My husband and I had boundless excitement and energy. I remember calling my parents and in-laws, baking bread from scratch, and going on a ten-mile bike ride. We were excited and on our way to having a little person call us "Dad" and "Mom." Immediately, we began to think about the future.

The nine months you're waiting for your baby to be born lend themselves to lots of discussions and plans for the future.

If you're in that excited, anticipatory stage, here's a list of some things to think about. (No expectant parents can decide everything at this point, but these are major questions to consider.)

- What do you want for your child? Pray together, dedicating yourselves to raising your child in the training and instruction of the Lord.
- What does God say about raising a family? Study the Bible together to find out.
- Does your church have classes for new parents? Check and see what's available.
- Does your church have a mentoring program for new moms and dads where you're paired with an experienced set of parents?
- How involved will you be in your local church? (If you haven't found a local church, what steps will you take to find one?)
- Are there differences in how you were spiritually trained? Maybe one of you grew up in a Christian home and one didn't. Or maybe one of you went to church only once a month, while the other was there every time the church doors were open. Maybe both of you grew up in Awana, but one was encouraged to learn the verses and one wasn't. All these things need to be discussed.
- Are you familiar with the church nursery? Volunteer to help. The staff will probably be glad to have you, and you'll become familiar with the other volunteers and the procedures.
- Can you be added to the church prayer list? Request prayer for wisdom as you raise your new child.
- Do you plan to set aside time as a family to study God's Word and pray, taking into consideration the ages of the children in choosing appropriate subject material?
- Will spiritual growth take precedence over other activities? Will your child miss a soccer game for church or church for a soccer game? Will you be just as diligent to work with a child on Bible memorization as you will be to teach him math?

Keep the answers to your questions in a journal or other special place. Yes, things change once that baby comes into the world—but discussing important subjects thoroughly now will help you be prepared when the situation is right in front of you.

AFTER THE BIRTH

Oh, the joy of a new baby—and the sleepless nights, the endless laundry, the constant diaper changes … and the unbelievable delight in holding that tiny person in your arms.

Study after study shows how important it is for an infant to bond with his or her parents. That's where the child finds safety and fulfillment of his needs. In forming that bond, you're creating an atmosphere that will eventually make understanding the love of the heavenly Father all the easier.

Here are some ways to get off to a good start:

- Pray with the baby before bedtime and meals. Even though the child can't understand, she becomes familiar with the pattern. Sometimes a child's first "spiritual" response is folding his hands before mealtime and then shouting "Amen" at the end of the prayer. Children don't truly understand what they're doing, but again, the parents are establishing a pattern that someday will be meaningful to the child.
- Read Bible biographies from bright-colored Bible storybooks. Even young babies enjoy hearing the sound of Dad's or Mom's voice, and looking at the appealing shapes and colors.
- Take your baby to church. Children who attend church from the beginning adjust better later on when attending age-appropriate classes. This also helps others in the church to become acquainted with your child.
- Ask a pastor or staff member to visit your home.
- Become acquainted with the children's ministries in your church.

PARTNERING WITH YOUR CHURCH

Be sure to look also at chapter 9 ("At the Starting Line") in part 2 of this book for ideas of how the church can partner with you at this stage in your child's life.

Notice especially the information there about a baby dedication service—where you stand before the church and publicly acknowledge that you want to raise your child in the training and instruction of the Lord (Ephesians 6:4). The congregation is usually asked to pray for you and your family.

CHAPTER 2

PRESCHOOLERS (AGES 2–5)

MASTER LIFE THREAD: RESPECT (GENESIS 39:6–9)

> *Train a child in the way he should go,*
> *and when he is old he will not turn from it.*
> PROVERBS 22:6

Several years ago, we laid new carpet on the stairway in our house—thick carpet, the kind that's fun to sit on, jump on, lie on, and curl your toes around.

One evening I was in the kitchen making supper when I heard unstoppable giggling punctuated by soft thuds. Curious, I walked into the hallway to find my two children making their way down the stairs on their bottoms.

"What are you doing?" I asked.

Gleefully, the two-year-old responded, "We're just bumping down the stairs with Jesus." He collapsed in another round of giggles.

That's a great example of how preschoolers perceive their heavenly Father—as someone who's right there beside them.

When my husband passed away a few years ago, our grandchildren were all preschoolers. As the adults grieved, the children were excited for Ken. "Grandpa gets to go to heaven. He gets to see Jesus. I think he's having a lot of fun, don't you? I wish I could go to heaven too." We had told them heaven is a wonderful place, and now that the reality of heaven was hitting our family in a sudden and life-changing way, the kids accepted it in the same spirit in which we had taught it. Why be sad about going to a wonderful place like heaven? In their own way, they encouraged us adults.

Yes, the preschool years are the time to build the foundations of a child's faith. These are the years when children form an initial understanding about God; His Son, the Lord Jesus Christ; and the Bible. They believe everything they're told about God. Why? Because we—the people they trust—are the ones who told them, and they unfailingly believe in us.

Preschoolers are limited not in *how much* they learn, but in *how* they learn it. They can't read. They can't study. They can't get themselves to church. They're totally dependent on parents or other close adults.

Think of the magnitude of our responsibility because of these limitations. We're the ones who choose what to teach them and, as a result, what they learn. Spiritual training is important at every age in life, but at no time is it more important than during these preschool years. They have no other access to the Bible except through us, the adults in their lives.

All parents teach their children *something* about God—though it might be that God is someone to be ignored, someone to be mocked, or someone whose name is a curse word. Whatever it is, they're teaching *something*.

As we've seen in the introduction, our desire is to raise children who reflect the same godly characteristics evident in the life of the biblical Joseph. (See Genesis 37—50.) And as we study Joseph's biography, we conclude that the foundational characteristic Joseph demonstrated was a *respect for the awesomeness and authority of God* (which includes respect for human authority).

Without this respect for God and His standards, a child cannot come to the point of salvation or make wise life choices.

> The fear of the LORD is the beginning of wisdom; all who follow his precepts have good understanding. To him belongs eternal praise. (Psalm 111:10)

By "fear," the psalmist didn't mean a cowardly terror, but rather an understanding of the awesomeness of God resulting in responsive, reverent obedience. Because we respect God, we want to do what He desires us to do.

Our goal is to teach our preschool child the hows and whys of respecting God.

We need to teach these truths:

- *God is the Creator* (Genesis 1:1). He created the flowers, the mountains, the kittens, the elephants. He created the stars way out in space. He created the entire universe. And He created the standard of righteousness.
- *God knows all* (Psalm 147:5). Preschoolers like *to know*. They're conscious of what they know and don't know. "I know my ABCs. Do you want to hear me say them?" "I know how to count to thirty. Wanna hear me?" They're also conscious that they don't know as much as their parents or their older brothers and sisters. Recently a five-year-old said to me, "I want to know how to read like my brother." Preschoolers are impressed with knowledge and can easily understand the concept that God knows everything.
- *God is everywhere* (Psalm 139:7–10). Preschoolers know they're in *one* place. They aren't at Grandma's house and at the doctor's office at the same moment. But God is everywhere. He's the only One who can be in all places at all times. That's a comforting thought to a child, because it means God is with each of us wherever we are.
- *God is different from us* (Psalm 90:2). We can understand from nature that God is powerful, creative, and personal (Romans 1:19–20). Beyond that, our knowledge of Him comes from His Word. He tells us everything we need to know about our past, present, and future. He tells us how we're to live our daily lives. But there are many aspects of God that He chooses not to tell us. God is *God*; we cannot understand everything that He understands and knows. Explaining to children how different God is from us can also help with those difficult questions of "Where did God come from?" and "How old is God?"
- *God is holy* (Psalm 77:13). *Holy* means set apart, perfect, and pure. In contrast to God's holiness, we are sinners; we're far from perfect. So God gives us instructions, guidelines, and laws on how to live the right way in light of His holiness. God sets the standard for what's right and wrong.

- *God is love* (John 3:16). Yes, God is the Creator of the entire universe, but He's also God of the individual. He loves each one of us.

The character of God isn't limited to these qualities. God is also *true* (Jeremiah 10:10); He is *faithful* (Psalm 100:5); He's *eternal* (1 Timothy 1:17); He's *all powerful* (Psalm 147:5); He is *just* (Psalm 11:7)—and the list continues on and on.

Teaching respect for God's awesomeness is a daily process. We communicate it not only through our words, but also through our actions. Do our children see us respecting our awesome God and responding in obedience? Or do they see us treating prayer, church, and Bible study as something "we *have* to do" before getting to the truly important or truly enjoyable tasks in life?

Begin each day with prayer, asking God to give you wisdom (and patience) as you convey His awesomeness and authority to your child.

WHAT THEY'RE LIKE:
CHARACTERISTICS OF PRESCHOOLERS

Preschool children are cute, wiggly, and in love with life. Their idea of a good time can be anything from jumping around the room (sometimes that's *all* they need to have a good time) to cuddling on the couch with Dad and Mom.

Many books have been written describing the characteristics of this age-group. We'll focus here on ten characteristics. Knowing them is pivotal in understanding how preschoolers acquire knowledge.

1. *Preschoolers are eager learners.* Every day they learn something new about life. Think about the helpless baby you brought home from the hospital just a few years ago. He couldn't do anything for himself except cry to let you know he was hungry, sleepy, or needed his diaper changed. Now, just a few years later, he runs, sings, recognizes his letters, does somersaults, and understands exactly how to melt your heart by sweetly saying "I love you" in the middle of a scolding.

Take advantage of his rapid ability to learn by giving him new experiences and teaching him new concepts and words. Teach him about the awesomeness of God. Stretch his young mind by presenting biblical concepts above and beyond the typical Bible "story."

2. *Preschoolers like to ask questions.* One way they learn is by asking questions—hundreds of questions. How many times has a parent heard "But why, Mom?" or "How come, Dad?" They have questions about everything, and we as adults can choose to deal with those questions either patiently or impatiently. When children ask those hard questions about God, we can remind them that God is different from us, that He knows everything, and that He's everywhere. We don't have to stumble around when being challenged by a four-year-old with "Where is God? What's He doing? How did He get to heaven?" Being patient listeners to our children *now* will encourage them to continue to come to us later with their tougher-to-ask questions without fear of being laughed at or ignored.

3. *Preschoolers watch and observe.* They learn by watching what other people are doing. That's why they pretend they're cooking dinner, going to work, or traveling on an airplane. They watch and they imitate. They also watch how Dad and Mom respond to tough situations. How many children have scolded a doll or stuffed animal using the same tone of voice or word choice a parent used on them?

But a child observes the good things too. Has your daughter taught a verse to her dolls, "like Daddy taught me"? Or played church? Or taught a younger brother or sister about Adam and Eve? Imitating older siblings or adults is part of their life education. If we want them to have a good attitude, a kind heart, and gracious speech, we need to model those characteristics for them.

4. *Preschoolers enjoy repetition.* They'll ask for the same book to be read to them over and over. They also have favorite DVDs they don't mind watching again and again. We can use this desire for repetition by repeating a verse or concept multiple times during the day. Reviewing is the key to learning, and preschoolers are natural reviewers.

5. *Preschoolers have fears.* Children can be afraid of dogs, thunder, monsters, new places, bugs, and various other things, some of which make no sense. (Unfounded fears in my own preschool brain included the moon, a reservoir, and a picture in the *Saturday Evening Post*.) What an excellent opportunity to emphasize God's constant presence.

Our encouragement should be that God is with us, helping us to be brave—not that He'll always protect us from the mean dog next door. What if the mean dog does escape one day and nips your child's leg? What if you do have a car accident? What if Grandpa does die? Did God forget to protect that day? God doesn't promise us immunity from bad things (Matthew 5:45; Romans 12:12), but He does promise to help us *through* all things.

6. *Preschoolers want the approval of adults.* Sometimes we're quick to show disapproval when a child does something wrong. Our emphasis should be on approval for what the child does right. As you teach

your child and he grasps a concept, give him a hug, a smile, a word of praise. Let him know you're excited that he learned a verse or remembered that God was with him during the thunderstorm. Children need to know that you approve of them and that you're excited that they're learning about trusting in the Lord.

Sometimes when children disobey or say something disrespectful, they're so "cute" in doing so that we laugh. Children notice and repeat the action or words because such laughter means approval. Giving approval for the right response is important, but we also need to watch that we aren't giving it for the wrong response.

7. *Preschoolers confuse real and make-believe.* As teachers and parents, we need to be clear in what is true and what is pretend. Preschoolers are literal thinkers. We say it; they believe it. Think how easy it is to convince them that a white-bearded man in a red suit flies a sled around the world, stops at every house, and eats tons of cookies, all the while delivering presents to a gazillion kids and still getting back home before dawn. Think how easy it is for parents to teach "respect" for Santa and to get kids to behave because Santa's watching them.

If parents consistently teach children (by word and example) that God is awesome and that He's with them at all times and in all places, preschoolers will believe. That's how they learn spiritual truth—through us, the adults.

That's a good reason for referring to Bible "stories" as Bible biographies—helping children know the difference between a "story" (implying "fictitious") and the truth. Even young children enjoy saying the word "biography" and can quickly understand that a biography is a true "story" about a person.

8. *Preschoolers love silliness.* God created them that way. So when they collapse in silly giggles because they stuck a hat on the dog or the baby has a piece of spaghetti stuck on her forehead, laugh with them. Remind them that God is the awesome Creator. He's so awesome that He created laughter. He wants us to have fun with our families. (Remember to thank God for laughter when you pray with your child.)

9. *Preschoolers understand right from wrong.* Any parent of a three-year-old can instantly discern guilt written on the face of a disobedient child. We need to teach our children what God says in His Word. We need to show them verses that command us to be honest, kind, and forgiving. Obedience to God is one way we show our respect for Him. Most children this age can't read, but we can still point out that the words come from the Bible. We have a reason for the rules we give our children—we want them to learn to do what *God* wants them to do.

10. *Preschoolers seek forgiveness.* They understand when they've done something wrong, and they want Dad and Mom to be happy with them (another aspect of seeking approval). Tell them about God's

righteous standard and our own inability to reach it. We're all born sinners, and we all sin. That's why God—our Creator and the One who knows all—understands that we need a Savior. That's why He sent His Son to die for us on the cross—so that our sins can be forgiven. That's the ultimate demonstration of forgiveness—an aspect of grace from our loving heavenly Father.

WHAT THEY'RE ASKING:
QUESTIONS PRESCHOOLERS HAVE ABOUT GOD AND THE BIBLE

Getting preschoolers to tell us their biggest question about God and the Bible was a challenge! Obviously, we couldn't have them write their questions on paper. And when we directly asked them, they responded, "I don't know." But parents and teachers were alert and sent preschoolers' questions to us one at a time.

Their questions centered around God or Jesus as a personal friend. They asked questions such as "Can You [God or Jesus] play with me?" or "Can You ride bikes with me?"

Other questions:

- Are You magic?
- How big are You?
- How do You know where we are?
- How did You make the sky?
- How did You make us?
- How did You make Yourself?

Although we give more detailed answers for some of the questions in the older age-groups, most of these questions can be answered by assuring the child that God is different from us and that He knows how to do everything. We can't know what God knows because we wouldn't be able to understand it—because we're not God.

Each of these questions can be answered by repeating the concept that God is awesome and deserves our love and respect.

WHAT YOU CAN DO:
SUGGESTIONS FOR TEACHING YOUR PRESCHOOLER TO *RESPECT* THE AWESOMENESS AND AUTHORITY OF GOD

What about Salvation?

Preschoolers *can* trust Christ as Savior, and many of them do. (I trusted Christ during the preschool years, and I truly meant and understood what I was doing.) Most children who make decisions at this young age come from strong Christian homes (as I did) where they're consistently taught God's Word. The concept of needing a Savior is a natural part of everyday discussion. These families usually attend church regularly where Dad's and Mom's words are backed up by teachers.

In other words, preschoolers (although I am sure there are exceptions) won't trust Christ after one family devotional time or one Sunday school class. Young children who respond to the gospel are hearing a consistent gospel message every day.

At the same time, we need to recognize we can often talk preschoolers into doing anything we want them to do or "believing" what we want them to believe. We, as parents and teachers, need to be very careful. We can explain what we mean when we talk about trusting Christ, but the initiative should come from the child herself. Or if the parent does take the initiative, he needs to be sure the child knows what she's doing.

Ideas and More Ideas …

Although not all of these ideas focus solely on the life thread of respect, they are valuable activities for the spiritual nurturing of your child.

1. *Attend meetings that introduce dads and moms to your church's vision for supporting parents as you spiritually nurture your children.*

2. *Attend your church's meeting for parents where staff members and experienced parents give ideas for spiritually training a preschooler.* Time may be set aside during this meeting for you to complete your family itinerary for the year. If not, fill out the itinerary at home.

As you develop your itinerary, remember the ages of your children. Preschoolers won't sit still while you read half the Bible to them, nor will they be able to memorize the entire book of Psalms. They can, however, do more than we sometimes think, so choose a good variety of attainable and challenging goals.

3. *Connect with a friend, family member, or church staff member to hold you accountable for pursuing your family itinerary.* (The church may arrange this for you.) Don't forget single parents. Can you do something to encourage them? Or if you're a single parent, make sure you connect with other parents. Ask a church staff member to help you if you're having difficulty finding willing accountability partners.

4. *Choose a family verse for the year.* It should center on respecting the awesomeness and authority of God. Choose a short one your preschooler can easily understand and memorize. Repeat it often. You might be surprised how much a young child can learn.

As director of our church's preschool, I wanted the three- and four-year-olds to know Scripture. At our first circle time, I simply stated the reference: "Psalm 23." The next day preschool was in session, I did the same thing. When I knew the children knew the reference, I added the first phrase: "The Lord is my shepherd." When they readily quoted those five words, I added the next phrase. By the end of the year, most of them could quote the entire psalm with no errors. The parents were amazed as they listened to their sons and daughters say the verses at our spring closing. We didn't push the children. We said the phrase just three times a week, and the kids got it.

5. *Ask teachers at church to provide you with lesson text and main points so you can review what your child has learned.* If the teacher has time, she could write out some questions that you could ask your child about the lesson. Discuss the lesson in casual conversation on the way home from church. If a child doesn't know an answer, review it. You don't want her to feel embarrassed at saying the wrong thing. The teacher might have used different words than you're using or used words beyond your child's understanding. Be positive. Don't get upset if your child didn't "get it"; simply teach it to her so she does "get it."

6. *Explain to your children that God is the Creator.* Only God can truly *create*—which means to make something out of nothing. Make something out of Play-Doh with your child. You could make a garden (garden of Eden) and shape some flowers and animals. Ask your child if you (and she) could make this garden out of nothing. Most preschoolers will respond that no, the garden is made from Play-Doh. Explain the difference between making a garden out of something and making one from nothing. Explain that when God created the earth, He made it out of nothing—He didn't use bricks or stones or Play-Doh. Only God can create like that. He is the wonderful, true God!

7. *Explain the meaning of character traits.* We talk about the character of God because we want to teach children what God is like, but children don't understand what we mean. Play a family game where you describe the other family members (only kind descriptions, of course). Remember that younger

preschoolers won't understand a lot of descriptive character words, so make sure your descriptions are age appropriate. "Mallory is happy. She always jumps around and giggles." "Daddy is strong." "Mommy is cuddly." "Daddy and Mommy know a lot."

When you see that your child understands what you mean, talk about what God is like. "Daddy is powerful, but God is even more powerful. He has all power." "Daddy and Mommy know a lot, but God knows everything." "Grandma is kind. God is kinder than anyone." "Our God is a great God!"

8. *Teach the definition of sin.* Not only do we do things that are wrong, but we're born sinners (Romans 5:19). No one had to teach your child to sin. No one had to teach your three-year-old to hit his baby brother in anger. No one had to teach your four-year-old to sneak behind your back and take the forbidden piece of candy from the counter. No one had to teach your five-year-old to selfishly grab a toy from a friend. Even young children can understand when they're doing wrong things. We need to teach our children that *sin* means thinking, saying, or doing anything that's disobedient to God. Teach your child that all people do wrong (even dads and moms). Only the Lord Jesus Christ is perfect (He cannot do wrong), and that's why He died for us.

9. *Go on family trips*—to the planetarium, the mountains, the oceans. Consistently remind your child that God is the Creator of everything you see.

10. *Take your children outside on a clear night.* Spread a blanket on the ground, lie back, and look at the moon and stars. If you can identify a planet, star, or constellation, do so. If you have a telescope or can borrow one, allow your children a closer look. Make the evening extra fun by roasting marshmallows or making s'mores. Recite one or two verses you've learned about God's creation. Pray together, thanking God for all He's done. Remind your children that you're looking at the same sun David wrote about in his songs (the Psalms).

11. *Make coloring impressions of God's creation.* Take a walk with your child. Collect flowers, leaves, grass, and twigs. Place your child's collection under tissue paper. Show her how to color over the paper with the side of a crayon, making an impression. Cut out the tracings, and glue them on a piece of construction paper. Write one of the praise verses your child has learned on the picture, and display it in a prominent place.

Or purchase solar-sensitive paper at a craft store. Help your child arrange the nature collection on the paper and put the picture in the sun. (Follow package instructions.) When you remove the nature collection, you'll see that the sun changed the color of the paper—except where the bits and pieces were lying. Your child's paper will now have a beautiful design.

12. *Teach your child that God made not only the things we see, but also the sounds we hear.*

- Check out a bird-song CD from the library. Listen to the birds in your yard. Can you identify them by their call?
- Check out a child's orchestra or band CD from the library. Look for one that features sounds from various instruments.
- Sing together. Remind your child that God created music.
- Listen to the wind. Take a walk in the park, and list the sounds you hear.
- Visit a petting zoo or a farm. Talk about the different sounds animals make. Imitate a cat's purr or a dog's bark.
- Talk about words. God gave us the ability to talk to one another. Ask your child what his favorite word is. (You might be surprised.) Ask him what words make him happy and what words make him sad.
- Visit the ocean or a large lake. Listen to the waves lapping at the shore and crashing against the rocks.

13. *Be consistent in your discipline.* Children need to learn the meaning of authority. As parents, we're the first authority figures in our child's life. We should expect children to immediately listen to our instructions and do what we ask. If we don't demand instant obedience, we're teaching that authority isn't important. If we laugh at a disobeying child (even though children can be funny), we're communicating that disobedience is a joke. Children need to learn that obedience to parents is the right way to respond. Only then can they understand the importance of respect and obedience to God.

14. *Sing.* Choose songs that praise God for His holiness, creation, or love, and sing them together as a family. Encourage your child to make up his own song of praise. Tell him to sing about things he's thankful for. The song won't rhyme, but you'll enjoy it (and I think the Lord will too).

15. *Teach your children the difference between telling the truth and telling a lie.* Sometimes we tell children not to lie, but we neglect to explain what lying is. Play a truth-and-lie game with them. As you're sitting at the supper table, make a true-or-false statement. Your conversation would go something like this:

You: I didn't eat a cookie. Is that the truth or a lie?

Child: A lie. I saw you eat the cookie.

You: Dad didn't go to work today because he was home sick. Is that the truth or a lie?

Child: Truth. Dad was sick today.

Play this now and then to teach your child to distinguish between true and false.

16. *Teach your children what it means not to steal.* Sometimes small children steal or shoplift because they don't understand that taking something from someone else is wrong. Our job is to teach them that stealing is a sin.

"You need to ask before you take something that belongs to Dad or Mom or your brothers." Or, "Things at the store belong to the store. You can't take something at the store without paying for it. That's wrong."

If your child is holding a piece of candy or a toy as you go through the checkout lane, insist he put it on the counter and make a big deal about giving your money to the clerk (or allow your child to hand the money to the clerk). You don't want your child to think he can pick up whatever he wants and get it for free.

Don't allow your child to bring a toy or book home from a church playroom or a friend's house—even if the person in charge or his friend's mom says it's okay (in response to the fit your child is having on the floor). Giving in will encourage him to scream again next time until he gets what he wants, even if it's not his.

17. *Explain that adults, too, must yield to authority.* God is our authority; you are your child's authority. Adults also need to listen to authority. We need to listen to bosses and to government officials. Remember, our children are watching. If we make fun of police for catching us going over the speed limit or running a red light, children will pick up on what we're saying. *We* need to show respect for authority if we want our children to show it.

Likewise, if our children hear us complain about Bible study or attending church, they won't take God's authority seriously. This is an area where we teach preschoolers by example.

18. *Teach children to sit still.* Do you dread church because your child constantly throws paper, eats candy, giggles, pokes his siblings, and makes countless demands to use the bathroom? You don't want church to be a battlefield, so train him early. We need to teach our children to sit quietly. Church is more than entertaining music and puppet shows. Eventually children need to know how to sit in a regular church service.

You want your child to listen and to allow people around her to listen too. That's why we need to teach and prepare our children to be respectful. Sitting quietly in church is a way to show respect to the pastor (or whoever is up front) as well as to the Lord. (Don't allow your child to parade out of church to use the restroom unless it's truly an emergency. Children walking in and out not only miss what's happening, but also disturb everyone else around them.)

To train your child at home, place him on a chair with a book or coloring supplies (no television) for five minutes. This isn't a punishment, and you don't want to treat it as such. Provide a special book or different crayons. Allow him to watch the clock click off the time. After five minutes, allow him to get up. Congratulate him for sitting still. Gradually extend the time until the child is able to quietly sit for thirty to sixty minutes. No, this isn't impossible. I know families that have done this with high-energy children, and it works.

Of course, meeting together for family worship is also training for sitting in church. However, often in family times, children are encouraged to spontaneously ask questions or to share in the discussion, so they aren't required to be as quiet as they are in church.

19. *Pray in front of your children.* Sometimes we choose rote prayers to pray with our children, but they need to know that prayer is talking to God about anything. They need to hear us pray about our jobs, our desire to be friendly to the neighbors, or our niece who's on a short-term missions trip.

Don't think they aren't listening. I still remember leading a group of teenagers in a prayer time when a three-year-old wandered in to join us. I put her on my lap, and she sat quietly as the teenagers prayed. Then Melissa whispered that she, too, wanted to pray, so we gave her opportunity. "Pray for Aunt Jane," she began in her sweet voice. "Give the doctors *wisboom.* Amen." I give the teenagers a lot of credit for not laughing, at least out loud—though we all smiled about it later.

We need to focus on thankfulness to God for the wonderful things He has done for us. We want our children to develop an attitude of thankfulness too. What better way to do it than to allow them to hear us be thankful in prayer?

20. *Eliminate distractions during prayer.* We sit down for a meal and start with thanking the Lord for the food. But the football game is still on in the background; big sister is in the other room talking on her cell phone; and the dog is chasing the cat around the house. We're talking to God, and we need to set a tone of awe and reverence for who He is and the privilege we have of communicating with Him. Teaching respect while talking to God teaches a child to respect God Himself.

21. *Keep a list of all the places you go in a week.* On a piece of construction paper, write a title that says "[child's name] Was Here." During the week, list everywhere your child goes: grocery store, library, church, preschool, babysitter's house, etc. Remind your child that God is with her in *all* those places. She can't go anywhere where God isn't.

22. *Teach that we learn about God's authority in the Bible.* The Bible is God's message to us. (Sometimes children will understand more easily if you compare the Bible to a letter God has written.) Children need to be taught that the Bible is how God speaks to us. This is important for all of us to understand.

Yes, during Bible times God spoke in burning bushes and through a hand writing on the wall, but those people didn't have God's written Word. We do. God's words are inside the Bible. Sometimes, even as adults, we miss this. We read a letter from a loved one who has died; the words are there, but they're from a person who's no longer alive. In contrast, the Bible is the *living* Word of God. He truly speaks to us through His Word as if He's sitting right here with us conversing (Hebrews 4:12).

23. *Read the Bible to your children.* You don't have to read entire chapters. Choose verses or a series of verses that your preschooler can understand. When you're teaching your child a memory verse, show her where the verse is in the Bible. Older preschoolers may be able to find the verse themselves or at least the book where the verse is located. If the verse is in John, write "John" on a paper, and encourage her to find where this is written on top of the page in her Bible.

24. *Teach your child that God loves her.* The awesome God who created the entire universe cares about your child. Thank God for His love when you pray. Be sure your child knows how important he is to God. Tell her God knows how many hairs are on her head. (Ask her to try counting them herself, to show how this task is impossible.) Point out a sparrow to your child. The Bible tells us that God knows when a sparrow is hurt (Matthew 10:29). If God cares about a sparrow, think how much He loves us.

25. *Encourage in your children an attitude of thankfulness toward others.* Children often understand the meaning of thankfulness by listening to people around them. You remind your child to say thank you to Mrs. Jones when she gives him a cookie. You say thank you to your child when she helps set the table.

When your child voluntarily says thank you, let him know you appreciate it, but don't overly praise him. Being polite should be a natural response. It's enough to smile and say, "I like to hear you say such kind words."

Even very young children can draw thank-you cards when a person has given them a gift. Require children to do this before they get busy playing with the toy. (Be sure to thank your child when she gives you a gift, even if it's a sweaty palm full of wilted dandelions.)

Connect thankfulness to the creation: "Thank You, God, for the sunshine." "Thank You, God, for the puppy." "Thank You, God, for Uncle Steve." "Thank You, God, for colors."

BIOS AND VERSES:
SUGGESTED BIBLE VERSES AND BIOGRAPHIES TO TEACH YOUR PRESCHOOLER

Here are some suggested Bible characters to study and verses to memorize, as you chart your family itinerary toward the life thread of *respect* for the awesomeness and authority of God.

If you have a say in your church's curriculum, you may want to coordinate these discovery topics and memory verses with what the church is focusing on in its teaching ministry to your child's age-group. Even if you aren't on the children's ministry team, you could suggest to your church to integrate these biographies and verses into its curriculum.

Biographies

1. *God as Creator* in Genesis 1. Creation is the very basis of a biblical foundation. God created everything from the stars in the sky to the tiny bug crawling across the sidewalk. God created a beautiful garden where everything was perfect. God is the Creator.

2. *Adam and Eve* in Genesis 2—3. Adam and Eve couldn't live up to God's perfect standard. They disobeyed God by eating from the forbidden tree—and therefore didn't meet God's standard even in resisting a piece of fruit. The simplicity of this sin is noteworthy. Of all the sins mentioned in the Bible, this one's so basic even very young children can understand it—taking forbidden food and, in doing so, violating God's law. God is holy. He sets the standard.

3. *Joseph* in Genesis 37:11–36; 39:2. Joseph was sold into slavery. Preschoolers can't completely understand the biography of Joseph, but they can understand parts of it. Joseph's brothers were jealous because of his coat (not so much because it had a lot of colors, but because it was made in the ornamental style of a prince or a person so rich he didn't have to work). Joseph's dreams also annoyed his siblings. Apparently there wasn't a lot of brotherly love in this family. Preschoolers can understand that Joseph was obedient to his father in checking on his brothers, that his brothers didn't like him (and

why), and that his brothers sold him to be a slave. (*Slavery* means that someone outside your family makes you work hard without pay.) Yet, Joseph knew God was with him.

4. *Heman* in 1 Chronicles 25:5–7. Heman and his family were the temple musicians. We don't read a lot about Heman, but he and his family provided the band music at the temple.

> God gave Heman fourteen sons and three daughters. All these men were under the supervision of their fathers for the music of the temple of the LORD, with cymbals, lyres and harps, for the ministry at the house of God. Asaph, Jeduthun and Heman were under the supervision of the king. Along with their relatives—all of them trained and skilled in music for the LORD—they numbered 288. (1 Chronicles 25:5–7)

Here's an account of a family that worked together and served God by praising Him at the temple. Does your family enjoy music? Tell your preschooler about Heman. Choose a few praise songs to sing together—make sure they're age appropriate for your child and that he can understand the meaning of the words. (Could your family offer to sing at church, a mission, or a nursing home?)

5. *Josiah* in 2 Chronicles 34. Josiah was a young boy who was crowned king. (His story can be an encouraging reminder that raising our own children in a godly home will affect future generations. Josiah was a very distant descendant of David, yet he walked in the ways of David, turning neither right nor left.) Relate Josiah's age to someone the children know. What a great truth to teach preschoolers—even a young child can know right from wrong and do great things for a great God.

6. *David* in Psalm 23. David is a need-to-know Bible character. Not only did he bravely battle Goliath, but he was crowned king of Israel, *and* Christ was born in the line of David. Unfortunately, we often emphasize the Goliath account and neglect to talk to our children about David's recognition of God's holiness. Choose verses from David's psalms that convey the magnitude of God's creation. Remind children that David saw the same sun, moon, and stars that we see. If your child likes to memorize, teach him all of Psalm 23. (Psalm 8 is another good one to learn.)

7. *Jesus* in Mark 4:35–41. The Lord Jesus Christ calmed the storm. As both God and the Son of God, He can calm wind and waves. He knows everything. He is all powerful.

8. *Jesus* in Luke 2; John 19—20. The birth of the Lord Jesus Christ, His death, and His resurrection *must* be taught to our children. The account of His birth is so familiar to us that we sometimes forget that many young children haven't heard it. Make sure you teach the correct facts to your children. So

much of what we hear is tradition rather than what the Bible actually says. (For instance, wise men didn't come to the manger, but to a house about two years after Jesus was born.) Children need to know that Christ came to earth because we're sinners in need of a Savior. Connect His birth in Bethlehem with the cross and resurrection.

9. *Jesus* in John 6:1–13. The Lord Jesus Christ fed the multitude with a young boy's lunch. This miracle (a *miracle* is something that can be done only by God's power) is one that children can understand—a large crowd is hungry, and the Lord Jesus multiplied the amount of food so everyone could eat (and there were plenty of leftovers!). Children relate because the Lord Jesus used the lunch of a child. Children can be reminded that God is different from us. His Son, the Lord Jesus Christ, can do things that no one else can do because He's divine and supernatural. The Lord Jesus was able to multiply the food because He is God, as well as the Son of God.

10. *Timothy* in 2 Timothy 1:5; 3:15. The biography of Timothy is an encouragement to both children and parents (and grandparents). Even as an adult, Timothy recognized the importance of what his mother and grandmother taught him. He learned about the same Old Testament characters that we're teaching our children. He learned about respecting the authority of an awesome God—as Paul reminded the young man Timothy with these words:

> Now to the King eternal, immortal, invisible, the only God, be honor and glory for ever and ever. Amen. (1 Timothy 1:17)

Memory Verses

Yes, preschoolers can memorize. Repeat the verses, make the learning fun. Play memory games with them.

Genesis 1:1. Creation is a child's introduction to God. Young children can understand that *create* means *to make out of nothing*. When your child builds a tower or plays with Play-Doh, she's using something that's already there to make something else. God is our Creator; the One who created flowers, apples, stars, giraffes, parents, and the entire universe. He didn't use blocks or Play-Doh. He made everything out of nothing. Understanding creation is the first step in understanding the awesomeness and authority of God.

Psalm 23:1. God is the God of the entire universe. God is the God of me. As David wrote, He "is my shepherd." Explain to your child that a shepherd is one who cares for sheep. Preschoolers are literal-minded thinkers and have difficulty understanding figurative speech. But most can understand the shepherd/sheep word picture. "We call God our Shepherd because He takes care of us like a shepherd takes care of his sheep."

Psalm 33:4. We learn what God is like (the character of God) in His Word. "The Bible is how God talks to us. His Word is right and true. Nothing in His Word is wrong."

Psalm 147:5. God's knowledge and understanding go on and on forever. We stand in awe as we think of all He's done. "God knows more than you. God knows more than I do. God knows more than Grandpa and Grandma. God knows more than everyone in the whole world put together. Because He knows everything, He's the authority over us."

Proverbs 3:5. Trust in God. What a great verse for a child to know as he faces the fears of life: thunderstorms, a barking dog, or being left with an unfamiliar babysitter. The focus here is that we can trust God to be with us at all times, not that everything always will turn out all right. We need to teach children that even in the scariest times, we can talk to God. He's our authority.

Matthew 28:20. This verse has a twofold message: We're to obey God's Word, and we can do so with the assurance that He's always with us no matter where we are. "God is with you when you go to preschool. He's with you when you come home. He's with you when you go to the park and when you go to the doctor. He's always, always with you. You can talk to Him wherever you are. He'll never go away."

John 11:25. God sent His Son, the Lord Jesus Christ, to earth so that He could die for us. Did you know He came alive again three days later? This is called the resurrection. We celebrate the Lord Jesus coming alive again in a special way at Easter, but the resurrection is important every day of the year. How amazing that God sent His Son for us! We have an awesome God.

Romans 3:23. All people are born sinners, and all people sin. Sin is anything we think, say, or do that God tells us not to think, say, or do. You've sinned. I've sinned. Aunt Cindy has sinned. Pastor Jeff has sinned. Everyone who has ever lived has sinned. So we cannot be good—without God. We need someone to save and rescue us from our sin. If your child knows about someone (or a pet) who was rescued in some way, remind him of that story to illustrate the word *rescue.*

Ephesians 6:1. I like to tell children that this is a commandment God wrote just for them. They're to obey (listen to their parents and do what their parents tell them to do). They don't have a choice. That's what they need to do because God is our authority and we need to listen to Him.

First John 4:10. God loves us so much He sent His Son, the Lord Jesus Christ, to earth to die for us. That's a lot of love!

WHAT NOT TO DO:
COMMON ERRORS TO AVOID WITH PRESCHOOLERS

"Don't run in God's house! God doesn't like it!" How many times have you heard parents snap those words at their three-year-old?

Unfortunately, threats are common from dads and moms of young children. This sounds like a great way to teach respect for God, but in actuality, parents use this terminology to keep their preschooler from doing what *they* (the parents) don't want him to do. Children learn that you aren't allowed to run, laugh, or have fun at church because God doesn't like it. The parents aren't teaching respect for God; they're making God the enemy.

Should kids run in church, outside of a gym or place where they're *supposed* to be running? Of course not, but tell them the real reason they shouldn't run. "Johnny, don't run in church because there are a lot of people. You might bump into someone and knock her down."

Don't blame God. Our bodies are the temples of the Holy Spirit; He's everywhere, not just in the brick building on the corner. Children should avoid running through the church auditorium because it's dangerous, not because they're in God's house.

I've also heard people tell their child, "Sarah, if you misbehave, I'll tell Pastor Smith on you." So, now the pastor becomes the enemy too. Again, don't blame the pastor for something *you* don't want your child doing. You want your child to respect the pastor and see him as a friend—someone she'll have a good relationship with as she grows older. You want her to be comfortable asking him questions or going to him if she has a problem she needs to discuss. Don't make him the enemy!

If you don't want your child to do something, then tell him the reason why rather than use idle threats.

CHECKLIST FOR PARENTS OF PRESCHOOLERS

This is a guide to help you, the parent, evaluate whether you need to emphasize a particular area in your child's spiritual growth. Use the lists below to gauge what areas you may have missed, so you can review those areas with your child. (Blank lines are included so you can add your own areas to review.)

Some of these statements are difficult to measure because they involve emotional responses (such as showing love and respect to God). Again, this list is a guide—not a test.

Knowledge Commitments

___ My child knows that God created the world.

___ My child knows that *create* means "made out of nothing."

___ My child understands that God knows everything and is everywhere.

___ My child knows that God is different from us.

___ My child knows that God is holy.

___ My child understands that God is our authority (the One who tells us what to do).

___ My child understands that Dad and Mom also have authority.

___ My child knows that God talks to us through the Bible.

___ My child knows that *sin* means thinking, saying, or doing anything that God tells us not to think, say, or do.

___ My child knows that the Lord Jesus Christ died for his or her sins and came alive again three days later.

(And others that you determine:)

___

___

Love Indicators

__ My child knows that God loved us so much He sent His Son, the Lord Jesus Christ, to die for our sins. My child desires to respond in love to God.

__ My child understands salvation. *(Remember that trusting Christ isn't something you want to force on your child, but be intentional about giving opportunities to respond to the gospel.)*

__ My child knows that prayer is talking to God, and my child participates when our family prays as a way of showing love to God.

__ My child has an attitude of thankfulness toward God.

__ My child desires to obey God because of love for Him.

__ My child desires to obey his or her parents.

__ My child enjoys attending church and learning about the Lord.

__ My child enjoys memorizing simple verses and understands that these are God's words to him or her.

__ My child has a good attitude about life.

__ My child displays godly qualities—such as truthfulness and kindness—because of love for God.

(Others:)

__

__

Service Activities

__ My child shows respect for God's creation.

___ My child sings songs of praise to God.

___ My child respects the possessions of others.

___ My child makes pictures and cards for people who are sick or who need cheering.

___ My child exemplifies obedience to parents and obedience to the Lord.

___ As I read from the Bible, my child listens to me (within an age-appropriate attention span) and can repeat to others what he or she has learned.

___ My child knows how to sit quietly in church and to not be a distraction to others.

___ My child shows kindness to others (such as an elderly neighbor).

___ My child talks to God in prayer.

___ My child willingly conveys thanks to others by words and actions.

(Others:)

___

___

THE FAMILY ITINERARY FOR FAMILIES WITH A PRESCHOOLER

Make this plan fit *your* family. Complete it at the beginning of each year while your child is a preschooler. While keeping a focus throughout this stage on respecting the awesomeness and authority of God, each year you should study different verses, biographies, and aspects of God's character. Don't forget to review what you learned in previous years.

Here are our spiritual goals for the year:

(Examples: That our child regularly prays, that we learn about six Bible characters, that we memorize five family verses, that our preschooler recognizes God as Creator, that we make a creation mural for the playroom, etc.)

1.

2.

3.

4.

5.

6.

Our family verse for this year is:

We'll also study the following six additional verses (one every two months) about God and His character:

    1.

    2.

    3.

    4.

    5.

    6.

We'll also study the following six Bible biographies (one every two months):

    1.

    2.

    3.

    4.

5.

6.

As a field trip in our study on the character of God, our family will go to ...

(This could be a hike up a mountain, a visit to a planetarium, a boat ride, etc.)

To reinforce an attitude of respect toward God, we'll also do the following activities together as a family:

(These could include field trips, craft projects, memory verses, etc.)

1.

2.

3.

4.

5.

6.

Our family has completed this year's family itinerary and met our spiritual goals.

(Have each family member sign.)

PARTNERING WITH YOUR CHURCH

Be sure to look also at chapter 10 in part 2 of this book for ideas of how your church can partner with you in the preschool years of your child's life.

Notice especially the information there about a "milestone celebration." This is a time for the church to honor those families that have reached their family itinerary goals. If your church is involved in a parent support program, it may present your family with a certificate of completion, and your older preschooler (who's ready to graduate into early elementary) may be awarded a children's Bible.

If your church doesn't participate in milestone celebrations, plan your own special event for your family to mark this milestone. Present your child with a children's Bible inscribed with a note from both parents, telling him your desire to see him grow into a young adult who truly knows, loves, and serves the Lord.

CHAPTER 3

EARLY ELEMENTARY
(AGES 5–8: KINDERGARTEN THROUGH SECOND GRADE)

MASTER LIFE THREAD: WISDOM (GENESIS 40:6–8)

My son, if you accept my words and store up my commands within you, turning your ear to wisdom and applying your heart to understanding, and if you call out for insight and cry aloud for understanding, and if you look for it as for silver and search for it as for hidden treasure, then you will understand the fear of the LORD and find the knowledge of God. For the LORD gives wisdom, and from his mouth come knowledge and understanding.

PROVERBS 2:1–6

The preschool Master Life Thread is *respect* for the awesomeness and authority of God. Part of that training included an understanding that the Bible is God's true, authoritative message to us.

But knowing a book's *author* doesn't mean one knows what the author says. Children must become familiar with Bible content, because this knowledge is the source of godly wisdom—as the above passage from Proverbs 2 points out.

Unfortunately, the trend in our society is to back away from Bible knowledge and center instead on experience and application. But application is impossible without something to apply. A *lot* of people have a *little* Bible knowledge. Your neighbor knows Noah built a boat and took a cruise with a bunch of animals but may have no idea why the flood happened in the first place or whether the whole event is fiction. Your friend understands that Christmas is a celebration of Jesus' birth but doesn't realize that the reason Christ came to earth was to rescue sinful humanity.

Sadly, many children (and adults) don't possess enough Bible knowledge to write a two-sentence summary.

One early elementary Awana club was planning a Noah's ark night. The children were told to dress up as one of the animals on the ark. This resulted in a very upset mom who said, "But my child only has a camel costume."

The leader explained that a camel costume was fine; there surely must have been camels on the ark. In fact, all animal costumes were acceptable.

But the mother protested. "I saw the movie, and there *weren't* any camels!" Nothing the leader said could convince this mom that camels were in the ark, because she didn't see the animals on the screen. Her child didn't show up that night.

To this mom, Noah was a movie, not a major event in the Old Testament. Unfortunately, her lack of understanding is all too common among church families, and it keeps them from tapping into the wisdom that's there for us in God's Word.

Proverbs is called the book of wisdom partly because it was written by the wisest man who has ever lived (talk about credentials!). Solomon painted beautiful word pictures about wisdom, such as this one:

> By wisdom a house is built, and through understanding it is established; through knowledge its rooms are filled with rare and beautiful treasures. (Proverbs 24:3–4)

Solomon was *the* VIP businessman of his time, accumulating wealth that would still be considered impressive. (No question—he'd be voted "Man of the Year.") But as a dad, he messed up. Morally, Solomon did what he wanted with no consideration of God's standards. Unfortunately, all the wise words that poured forth from Solomon's mouth meant nothing to his children, who observed the man behind the words.

We can learn from Solomon. Knowledge must be taught *and* lived for wisdom to result.

When we asked early elementary children to give us their biggest question about God and the Bible, they asked for the details. They wanted to know the what, why, and how of Bible events. They *desire* knowledge—and children this age can absorb a *lot* of knowledge. Some educational philosophies even call this the "information dump" age, because kids absorb so much. Every day brings new discoveries of words or concepts.

Our responsibility as parents is to ensure that the knowledge we give them isn't just fluff and stuff, but godly knowledge that results in godly wisdom.

Only when children comprehend the magnificence of *who God is*—and the remarkable realization that the Bible is God's *living* Word—will their hearts reproduce the godly response of love and service.

WHAT THEY'RE LIKE:
CHARACTERISTICS OF KINDERGARTEN TO SECOND GRADERS

Early elementary children enjoy learning. They're old enough to understand that they don't know as much as their older brothers and sisters. They want to ride their bike around the block, ride in a car without needing a "baby" car seat, and read chapter books. They ask questions about the stars and anteaters and whether or not *we* would have sinned if *we* were Adam or Eve.

We can capitalize on that love of learning by not only teaching them and training them, but wisely guiding them in making good choices.

Let's consider ten characteristics of this age-group that are pivotal in helping us understand their learning process at this point in their childhood:

1. *They're transitioning from "little kid" to "grown-up kid."* They're now attending school (either away from home or in the home), reading, having playdates, and maybe joining a soccer or baseball team. They enjoy thinking of themselves as "big kids."

We can capitalize on that as we teach: "I need you to think real hard. This is something that's difficult to understand, but I know you're smart enough to do it: Why do you think Joseph's brothers didn't like him? Why do you think they were jealous of his coat?"

Instead of telling them all the answers, challenge them to come up with their own—though we as parents need to make sure their answers are correct. If their answer is incorrect, we need to guide them toward coming up with the correct one.

Interestingly, just this morning I was talking to a young mom who told me about an article she had recently read that was lamenting the lack of critical thinking ability in children who are otherwise well educated.

Even kids as young as early elementary age can be taught to think. We need to appeal to their desire to understand just about everything.

2. *They're perfectionists.* Many children this age tend toward perfectionism. Their desire is to do a good job reading, coloring, playing games, or saying verses. One eight-year-old told me she wanted to write stories, but she was fearful she didn't know how to spell all the words she wanted to use. Her solution? Not writing anything at all.

When children can't do something exactly right, they become frustrated. That frustration can lead to tears, anger, or refusal to continue with the project. *Wisdom is persisting until a job is complete.* God likens our job responsibility to an ant (Proverbs 6:6). Why not do some research on ants with your child?

Teach perseverance and patience. We can help and encourage and remind our children that God wants us to do our best, but only He is perfect.

3. *They're sensitive to criticism.* This correlates with the perfectionist characteristic. Emily's drawing a picture for Aunt Heather. Big brother walks by and laughs. "Your kitten looks like a sick whale." Or little brother walks by and rips off a corner of the page. Both intrusions into Emily's world immediately have her in tears. She doesn't want to be criticized. She wants her drawing to be exactly right. Again, you need to reassure her of your love and of God's love.

This doesn't mean parents can't point out what a child has done wrong. Too many parents worry about their child's self-esteem to the point of convincing the child he's perfect.

We're sinners and we need correction, but the criticism should be focused on the action, not the child.

Incorrect: "Emily, I told you to clean up your room, and you didn't. You're a stupid kid and won't ever amount to anything. I give up." (You might think my illustration is harsh, but that's exactly how many parents—even Christian parents—talk to their kids. And many throw in swearwords as emphasis.)

Correct: "Emily, I told you to clean up your room, and you didn't. Because you didn't obey, you won't be allowed to go to Madison's house this afternoon. Instead you'll spend the time straightening up your room. That's final." (And that should be final. No argument. No attack on the child. No debate. No further discussion.)

4. *They worry.* A child this age is learning that the world is bigger than home, Grandma's house, pre-school, and church. They begin to worry about things. Will a tornado hit me? Will my dog die? Will Dad and Mom get a divorce? (I've heard children as young as three discuss these things.) Remind them of the awesomeness of God. He's everywhere. He knows everything. He has all power. We can trust in Him.

5. *They like rules.* Last night as we were sitting down to supper, the three-year-old decided he wanted to sit where the second grader usually sat. The second grader was not about to let it happen; that was *her* seat and always had been, and she wasn't about to change *now.* Mom's response was to give a third child—the kindergartner—permission to tell people where to sit, since she had set the table. The kindergartner assigned each of us a chair—exactly where we always sit (much to the glee of the second grader). "Because," she said, "these are the sitting rules." They like order. Remind them of God's authority and that the Bible is where we read about the rules He has for us.

6. *They like consistency.* Because they appreciate consistency and because they're observers, they're quick to point out inconsistencies in others. "Dad, you shouldn't be eating that. You need to eat healthy. My teacher said fried chicken isn't healthy." "Mom, you said I couldn't go outside without a jacket. Then why aren't you wearing a jacket?"

Sometimes their questioning can be disrespectful. We need to counteract with wise words, reminding them that Dad and Mom have the authority to be in control. Dad usually does make good eating choices. Mom can go outside without a jacket because she's wearing a warm sweater or simply because she isn't cold.

We can use this desire for consistency in our teaching. We need to remind them that God's laws and standards are always consistent. Lying isn't wrong on Monday and right on Tuesday. Kindness is always right. Stealing is always wrong. Sometimes we (dad, mom, teacher) make mistakes that mess up our lives, but God *always* does what He says.

7. *They enjoy stories.* They like to read them and listen to them. But they also want to know which stories are true and which are made up. Often after telling a story to a first grader, the child will ask, "Did that really happen?" That's why the word *biographies* is a good substitute description for a Bible "story." Children can be taught that biographies are true.

Children can understand the following descriptions. You may want to preface any story you tell with one of these statements:

- This story is made up.

- This story is a Bible biography. Everything about the story is true because it's from God's Word. (Parables, of course, are made-up stories with a true point—from the Bible.)
- This story is true, but it's not from the Bible. This happened to me when I was a child.

We strengthen a child's belief system when we distinguish between truth and fiction.

8. *They have great memory skills.* They can memorize songs, phone numbers, addresses, stuffed-animal names, and plots of television shows. Encourage them to use their memory skills to work on learning God's Word. Challenge them. You might be surprised at how much they're able to memorize.

9. *They double their speaking capacity.* These children enjoy learning big words. Take advantage of that, and teach them big words from the Bible. Sometimes we tend to talk down to them, but we shouldn't. For instance, teach them that *inspiration* means that God told the men who wrote the Bible what He wanted them to write. Review the word *inspiration* over and over. They enjoy knowing and defining what they've learned.

10. *They learn by seeing and doing.* We know children have different learning styles, but no matter what their basic learning style, children in the early elementary years are surrounded by media. Learning the letter *K* involves watching a personified, sparkly red *K* dance across the television screen or hearing music play when you match two *K*s correctly while playing a computer game.

That doesn't mean everything we teach these children needs to be media oriented. In fact, we should encourage quiet times of learning. Children still enjoy listening to Dad read a story or memorizing a verse with Mom. But we need to be aware that the majority of children today are being conditioned to be visual learners.

WHAT THEY'RE ASKING:
QUESTIONS KINDERGARTEN TO SECOND GRADERS HAVE ABOUT GOD AND THE BIBLE

We asked children in this age-group, "What's your biggest question about God and the Bible?" They thought. They looked at the floor. They looked at the ceiling. They looked around. And then they told us.

The most-asked questions from this age-group centered on the Lord Jesus Christ. In fact, the number one question is why did Jesus die? Children were curious about the details of Christ's birth, death, and resurrection. This trend in questioning is significant, because many children trust Christ in the early elementary years.

Here are a few of the top questions asked by children in this age-group (not including the many requests for details about specific Bible characters)—plus some help with the answers.

1. *Why did Jesus die?*

God sent His Son, the Lord Jesus Christ, to earth as a man because we needed Him to take the punishment for our sin. He became human, but He was different from us because He is perfect. He didn't sin. He couldn't sin. He is the Son of God (John 3:16; 5:24; 1 Corinthians 15:3–4).

2. *Why did God create people?*

- God created us to love Him (Deuteronomy 6:5).
- God created us to honor Him (Psalm 139:14).
- God created us to serve Him (Matthew 25:40).

3. *Where did God come from?*

John 4:24 tells us God is a Spirit. He didn't come from anywhere—He always was. The Lord Jesus is a person with skin and bones. He was physically born in Bethlehem. God wanted to come down and live with us and then die for us to save us from our sins. Jesus is God's Son, and Jesus is God, and He always was and always will be.

And Acts 17:27 says that people should seek the Lord. He's not far from any of us. Because God didn't come from anywhere, we don't have to go anywhere to find Him. At any time, we can pray to Him and know that He can hear us. We're not alone.

4. *What does heaven look like?*

- We'll live in a perfect place where God is the King (Revelation 21:4).
- We'll receive new and perfect bodies in heaven (2 Corinthians 5:1–5; 1 Corinthians 15:40–44).
- We'll have a new and perfect purpose (Revelation 5:13; 22:5).

And I heard a loud voice from the throne saying, "Now the dwelling of God is with men, and he will live with them. They will be his people, and God himself will be with them and be their God. He will wipe every tear from their eyes. There will be no more death or mourning or crying or pain, for the old order of things has passed away." He who was seated on the throne said, "I am making everything new!" Then he said, "Write this down, for these words are trustworthy and true." (Revelation 21:3–5)

5. Why does God love us?

God loves us because God is love. That's who He is. His very nature is love.

Do we deserve His love? No, we all disobey Him and forget about who He is and what He tells us to do in His Word, the Bible (Jeremiah 17:9; Romans 3).

He created us and desires for us to be His children (1 John 3:1). He loved us when we were still sinners (Romans 5:8; 1 John 4:9).

WHAT YOU CAN DO:
SUGGESTIONS FOR TEACHING YOUR KINDERGARTEN TO SECOND GRADER THAT *WISDOM* FOR LIFE COMES FROM KNOWING GOD AND HIS WORD

What about Salvation?

Has your child trusted Christ?

Many children trust Christ as Savior between kindergarten and second grade. Often they have parents who consistently stress the importance of the gospel, and those conversations are backed up by teachers at church.

(If your child trusts Christ at a church event, talk with the teacher and find out what lesson was taught, etc. Finding out as much as you can also helps you talk to your child about what he's done.)

Children in this age-group are sensitive. They know they do wrong. They also have a desire to know about the Lord and what He's done for us. We need to take advantage of their interest and teach about God's great love.

Because I trusted Christ at a very young age, I've often shared my experience with children. I tell them that I knew I had sinned by disobeying my parents. I knew that the Lord Jesus had to die on the cross so those sins could be forgiven. I tell them how excited I was when I became a Christian because that meant I would go to heaven someday. They giggle when I tell them I was saved in the bathroom (while my mom was drying my hair). They listen because hearing about a teacher's childhood experience is always fun for them—and a good way for both parents and teacher to teach.

When your child trusts Christ, record it in the front of her Bible. Write down the date, place, time, and circumstances. This gives the child tangible evidence if she later doubts her salvation.

Ideas and More Ideas …

Although not all these ideas focus solely on the life thread of wisdom, they're valuable activities for the spiritual nurturing of your child.

1. *Attend meetings that introduce dads and moms to your church's vision for supporting parents as you spiritually nurture your children.*

2. *Attend your church's meeting for parents where staff members and experienced parents give ideas for spiritually training early elementary–age children.* Time may be set aside during this meeting for you to complete your family itinerary for the year. If not, fill it out at home as soon as possible.

As you develop your itinerary, remember the ages of your children. But don't underestimate their capabilities. Children at this age can absorb a lot, especially if you include opportunities for review.

3. *Choose a family verse for the year.* Unless you have a child who truly has difficulty learning, don't be concerned about the length. Children at this stage are good learners and can memorize several verses if Dad and Mom are memorizing and working with them.

4. *Join a small group, Sunday school class, or parenting class.* You'll be encouraged by talking with others who are traveling through the same stages of parenting as you are. If your child has a friend whose parents have created their own family itinerary, your families could team together and enjoy joint activities. (For instance, visit the Creation Museum in Kentucky, or write and put on a play about a Bible character with different family members playing the different roles.)

5. *Ask what your child is learning at church.* Question your child about what she learned, and suggest that she retell the lesson to you or to her younger siblings.

6. *Reinforce what your child learned during her preschool years.* Respect for the awesomeness and authority of God is something we need to remember all through our lives. Visit places that have different types of scenery—forests, parks, mountains, lakes, etc. Remind your child that God is the Creator of all things.

Give your child a small garden plot, and allow him to plant flowers or vegetables. Show him how to water and weed. Remind him that each plant is a miracle of God's creation—a flower or a carrot from one tiny seed.

7. *Teach your child the books of the Bible.* Explain why you want her to learn them. "Knowing the books is like having a map to God's Word. By learning the books, we know if a verse is at the beginning or at the end of the Bible. We know if the book is in the Old Testament or New Testament."

Make the learning process fun (instead of a chore). Use songs and repetition. Talk about the funny-sounding names. Talk about why the books have the names they do. Some of the funniest sounding ones are people's names!

See how quickly your child can say the books. Show your child how quickly *you* can say them.

8. *Explain the difference between a book, a chapter, and a verse.* Once your child knows how to read, give him a Bible reference and see if he can find it. Choose verses that he knows from memory. Tell him that chapters are parts of a book and that verses are parts of a chapter.

My granddaughter often sits with me in church. If a verse is mentioned from the pulpit, I challenge her to look it up. Not only does she have a sense of pride when she finds it, but she's learning good habits for the future.

9. *Teach the difference between a wise and a foolish choice.* Wise choices are made when we listen to God's instructions. Foolish choices are made when we ignore God's instructions. The next time your child struggles with a decision, ask her to determine whether the choice is wise or foolish. Some choices are hard. A child may be invited two different places at the same time. You've left the choice up to her, and maybe there isn't a right or wrong to the issue. Guide her in making wise decisions. Talk about Bible characters who made wise choices and those who made foolish choices.

10. *Buy a Bible storybook that goes through the Bible chronologically.* You want one that's appealing to children and biblically accurate. Read the verses about the person or event from the Bible; then read the "story" from the book.

Don't stop with reading—do some further research. In your yard or at a park, measure off the size of Noah's ark. (You might be surprised!) Or figure out how many pennies make up a shekel. Bake unleavened bread. Be excited about teaching your child the Bible!

11. *Choose a Bible character, and learn everything you can about him or her.* For instance, choose Barnabas. What does his name mean? Where does he live? What did he do? Why and where is he talked about in the Bible? What places did he visit with Paul? (Find them on a map.)

12. *Encourage your child to role-play events from the Bible.* Occasionally make a big production (well, big for the inside of your house, anyway). Make a background. Design costumes from fabric. Put the play on for grandparents, neighbors, or anyone you can find who will watch.

13. *Make a DVD with your child.* He dresses up as someone in the Bible and then acts out the event as you record it. For instance, he could be David. Perhaps you could find a friendly farmer who has a field of sheep. Your child could "play his harp," practice his slingshot (though not aiming at the farmer's sheep), and pretend he's writing a psalm using a small stone on a bigger rock. Be creative! These are the kind of adventures your child will remember.

14. *Choose a Bible character (with your child's input).* Ask your child to write what she thinks it would've been like to be that person. (You may need to have your child dictate while you do the writing.) How did knowing God help the person in her life? How did the person use wisdom in making life choices?

15. *Show your child pictures of Israel or other places where Bible events took place.* A quick search online can bring up dozens of pictures. Or there may be someone in your church (or a family or friend) who has been to Israel. Invite him over for supper, and ask him to show the pictures to your family. (Remember, early elementary–age children don't have long attention spans, so show a few pictures of the place you're studying from the Bible—not a three-hour home-video rendition of every hill or temple.) Seeing real pictures of real places will help your child comprehend that these events happened.

16. *Purchase a cookbook from Israel* (or another Bible location such as Egypt or Greece), or get recipes from the Web. Prepare a meal that uses some of the ingredients mentioned in the Bible or fruits grown in the Middle East.

17. *Encourage your child to memorize.* Children this age memorize quickly. Further their enthusiasm by learning verses with them. Choose a passage of Scripture that tells of a Bible event or character. Acts 16:16–31 is one example. Or, choose ten verses on wisdom from the book of Proverbs.

18. *Play games using Bible characters.* After your family has studied the lives of several people, secretly choose one. Children ask yes-or-no questions until your children guess who it is. Allow them to have a turn choosing a character, and you guess who it is.

19. *Buy a roll of newsprint or tablecloth paper.* Cut a long length of paper, and divide that paper into segments. Ask your child to draw in each segment a scene from the life of a Bible character. Unless you have an overly enthusiastic artist, do this over a period of several days or even weeks.

20. *Read a missionary biography to your child.* Talk about the wise choices made by the missionary. Why were those choices sometimes difficult? How did he or she use wisdom?

21. *Teach (and show by your own words) the importance of wisely chosen words.* Children this age hear words and don't always understand what they mean. They may try out a new word at the dinner table (usually when guests are present), horrifying everyone.

Give your child the freedom to say a word once for the purpose of definition. If you say the word is unacceptable (you may choose not to define it), the child isn't permitted to say the word again. Other times you'll find the word isn't inappropriate at all; it's just a word the child hasn't heard before.

By allowing him the opportunity to ask about the word one time, you can stop him from innocently using inappropriate language. You also teach him he has the freedom to come to you when he hears things from his friends that he doesn't understand.

22. *Watch children's television programs or DVDs before allowing your child to watch them.* Set up criteria beforehand, and tell the child he won't be allowed to watch if the show isn't within those standards. Familiarize your child with your guidelines. Criteria could include the following: Do the people in this show use bad language? Do they make fun of God or the Bible? Do they get things by lying (without consequences)? Do the children make fun of or talk back to their parents? (You might want to watch two or three episodes before making a final decision.)

Then tell your child exactly why you like or don't like the program. This way you're training him to judge for himself whether or not a show is appropriate. Someday he'll be asked to watch something and you won't be there—whether he's at a friend's house or seeing something at school. Eventually he'll have to make his own decisions.

If you know enough about the show to know it's not inappropriate, you may want to include your child in the first-time viewing and ask him to help you judge whether it's good or bad.

23. *Purchase a child's book on customs in Bible times.* Being familiar with how things were done will help a child gain knowledge and understanding of the Bible. For instance: Why did everyone wear sandals? Why would you give myrrh as a gift? What is "gleaning"? What was their money like back then? Did their kids go to school? Did they play games, or did they have to work all the time?

24. *Pray with your child.* Make your prayers conversational, focusing on thankfulness for all you have. Pray for wisdom in making choices. Pray for enthusiasm and a desire to learn more of God's Word. (Have you ever encouraged your child to thank God for the privilege of memorizing the Bible? Or have you encouraged him to pray for desire to learn his memory verses?)

25. *Compose a song or poem about a Bible character.* Work together as a family writing a song about Moses or Joshua (or any other Bible character). Include in the song what that person did and how God

showed His power to that person. If someone in your family is musical, you can put music to the lyrics. Perhaps you could perform it at the end-of-year milestone celebration.

BIOS AND VERSES:
SUGGESTED BIBLE VERSES AND BIOGRAPHIES TO TEACH YOUR
KINDERGARTEN TO SECOND GRADER

For looking closer at Bible characters and for memorizing verses, here are suggestions to get you started as you chart your family itinerary toward the *wisdom* based on knowing God and His Word.

You may want to coordinate these discovery topics and memory verses with what your church is focusing on in its teaching ministry to your child's age-group.

Biographies

1. *Joseph* in Genesis 37—50. Review his story. Emphasize his early family life, why his brothers hated him, and the result of that hate. Highlight some of the major events that happened during the rest of his life. Through every situation, Joseph understood that God was with him. "Then Pharaoh said to Joseph, 'Since God has made all this known to you, there is no one so discerning and wise as you'" (Genesis 41:39).

2. *Noah* in Genesis 6:9—9:19. Noah obeyed God even when everyone around him disobeyed. He displayed wisdom in building an ark even though doing so in a rainless land seemed to make no sense. No one outside his family listened to him, yet he did what was right.

3. *Moses* in Exodus 1:1—2:10; Acts 7:22. Moses was raised in the palace and became wise in the ways of the Egyptians. Yet as an adult he made the life-changing choice of listening to God and leading God's people, the Israelites, out of Egypt. Not all his choices were wise ones, but he understood God's sovereignty.

4. *Joshua and Caleb* in Numbers 13. Joshua and Caleb were two of the twelve spies sent into the Promised Land of Canaan. Ten came back grumbling about the giant people and the walled cities. Only Joshua and Caleb understood that the awesome God who had brought them this far would continue to help them. Even though Joshua and Caleb were right, the people chose to listen to the "foolish" spies

who weren't trusting God. God honored Joshua and Caleb's faith by allowing them to enter the Promised Land.

5. *Joshua* in Joshua 10:1–13. Joshua spoke to the sun, and God caused the sun to stop. Joshua once again made a good choice and willingly fought a fierce enemy. This part of Joshua's biography shows not only that he was willing to obey God, but also that God has the ultimate authority. When Joshua told the sun to stand still (so the enemy couldn't hide in the darkness), God showed His authority by causing that to happen.

6. *Solomon* in 1 Kings 3:3–15; 4:29–34; 10:1–13. God spoke to Solomon in a dream and offered Solomon whatever he wanted. Although Solomon was young and he could have asked for wealth, fame, or power, Solomon asked for wisdom. That's exactly what God gave him. In fact, Solomon became the wisest man of all time. Solomon knew a lot about wisdom, but he didn't always make wise choices.

7. *Shadrach, Meshach, and Abednego* in Daniel 1:20; Daniel 3. The Bible tells us that these three men were wise: "In every matter of wisdom and understanding about which the king questioned them, he found them ten times better than all the magicians and enchanters in his whole kingdom" (Daniel 1:20). They weren't afraid to worship the true God even when everyone else was worshipping an idol. Even the threat of being thrown into the fiery furnace didn't stop them from doing what was right. (As your child gets older, use these three men as an illustration of good peer pressure. All three made the right choice *together*.)

8. *The magi* in Matthew 2. These wise men started with earthly wisdom and ended with the wisdom that comes only from God. (Review the events of the birth of Christ leading up to the wise men.) The magi didn't come to the manger, but to Joseph and Mary's home sometime later. The time is significant because it shows the effort (in time taken) they needed to put forth to travel a great distance to honor the new King.

9. *Jesus* in Matthew 19:13–15. The Lord Jesus wanted the parents to bring their children to Him. The disciples had a problem with that. They thought Jesus had more important things to do and chased the children away. They didn't understand how much the Lord Jesus loves children and how much He values them. Tell your child how much you love her, and remind her that Christ loves her so much He died on the cross for her sins. Emphasize that He once again came alive. He didn't stay dead but is preparing a home for us in heaven.

10. *Paul* in Acts 9:1–29. Paul met the Lord Jesus Christ on the way to Damascus. He was on his way to persecute (be mean to) the Christians. Before he met Christ, he was wise in things that didn't

make a difference. After he met Christ, he became excited about telling others about Christ. In fact, he wrote that he was to preach to the wise and the foolish—all people.

Memory Verses

Joshua 1:9. Your children are getting older. They're going places and participating in activities that give them a new window on the world: school, soccer, art classes, a friend's house, etc. Remind them that God, the Creator of the universe, cares about them. He's willing to give them courage no matter where they are or what they're doing. God doesn't promise to give us easy lives, but He *does* promise to give us strength and courage when we face hard situations—and understanding this is an aspect of wisdom all Christians need to learn. This verse, along with Hebrews 13:6 (see below), offers words of wisdom we need to carry in our hearts.

Psalm 119:105. Children this age memorize quickly and are good learners. This is the age when we need to teach them the details of the Bible. Wisdom based on biblical knowledge can guide them through the ups and downs of life.

Proverbs 2:6. The world finds false wisdom in fame, money, and power. But these kinds of "wisdom" eventually fail. True knowledge, understanding, and wisdom come from God.

Proverbs 15:33. We teach our children to "fear" the Lord and to respect His awesomeness and authority. From that understanding comes wisdom.

Proverbs 20:11. Children may think they're too young to serve God. *We* may think they're too young to truly understand God. Young children reflect who they are in mind and heart by their actions. Even young children are testimonies of God's love and grace.

John 3:16. Our awesome heavenly Father—the Creator of the universe, all powerful and all knowing— loves each one of us. He loves us so much He sent His Son to die for our sins. This is the message of God's Word. To know and then believe the message of this verse is the greatest wisdom of all.

John 20:31. Children at this age like to learn, and God gave us the Bible so we *can* learn. The basis of biblical learning is knowing who God is and that the Lord Jesus Christ is the Son of God. If we believe in Him and what He's done for us on the cross, we'll receive the gift of eternal life.

First Corinthians 15:3–4. Good verses for everyone to know. This is a two-verse summary of the gospel.

Hebrews 13:6. Like Joshua 1:9, this is a particularly good verse for this age-group. Is your child having a difficult time in school or being bullied by kids in the neighborhood? Write the words of these verses on a small piece of paper, and stick it in your child's lunchbox or pocket so he can remember that God is with him. Even if your child doesn't read, he can memorize the verses, and the paper can be a reminder to him.

James 2:10. In our own wisdom, we can look back at Adam and Eve and say, "I wouldn't have disobeyed God!" Or we can look at other people and say, "I'm not *that* bad!" But we're *all* sinners. Breaking even one of God's laws makes us guilty of breaking them all. Wisdom is acknowledging our need for a Savior.

WHAT NOT TO DO:
COMMON ERRORS TO AVOID WITH KINDERGARTEN TO SECOND GRADERS

Many parents are experts at giving their children sermons—in the middle of punishment. "Joey, you spilled your milk! *I can't believe how clumsy you are!* What a mess! God doesn't like that! You're making God unhappy. He doesn't like you making extra work for Mom!" These words are usually snapped at the child as he cowers in the corner. The parent might think he's teaching his child about God—and he is. But he's teaching that God is a threat, a verbal weapon to use in the midst of anger. Seldom do we use wise, kind, and instructive words when we're frustrated.

Part of our responsibility is to teach our children the definition of sin. But this instruction needs to come when we're calm, not in the midst of an adult temper tantrum. We need to think about the messages we convey to our children. (By the way, occasionally spilling milk isn't a moral wrong; it's a kid being a kid. Adults spill things too.)

Another mistake is praying about a child's sin in front of others. Dad prays at the supper table, "Dear Lord, please help Andrew not to steal any more money from my wallet, and make Jacob quit goofing off at school, and help Lauren to stop hanging around with that wild kid across the street." A parent may think this public humiliation will help his children do right, but Dad's only embarrassing his children and making them dislike him, God, and prayer.

Sure, we should pray with our children about their choices, but the prayers should be prayed in private, not in front of family and friends. And the prayers should be prayed in love, not to instill guilt.

Our desire is for our children to recognize they're sinners and, as a result, to turn to God—the God of grace and forgiveness.

CHECKLIST FOR PARENTS OF KINDERGARTEN TO SECOND GRADERS

This is a guide to help you, the parent, evaluate whether you need to emphasize a particular area in your child's spiritual growth. Use the lists below to gauge what areas you may have missed, so you can review those areas with your child. (Blank lines are included so you can add your own areas to review.)

Some of these statements are difficult to measure because they involve emotional responses (such as showing love and respect to God). Again, this list is a guide—not a test.

Knowledge Commitments

___ My child remembers the truths learned about God during the preschool years. *(Review the preschool checklist.)*

___ My child knows that the Bible is the true and authoritative Word of God.

___ My child knows that the Bible is God's message or letter to us.

___ My child knows that Bible characters were real people and that the events of the Bible happened in real places.

___ My child knows the books of the Bible.

___ My child knows how to locate books in the Bible, to pronounce their names, and to give an overview of the Bible's theme.

___ My child can identify at least twenty-five Bible characters.

___ My child knows there are some questions that only God can answer—they're the "secret things" that belong to the Lord (Deuteronomy 29:29).

___ My child can explain how to trust Christ.

___ My child knows what the Bible says about heaven.

(Others:)

—

—

Love Indicators

— My child responds to God's love by showing love to others.

— My child understands that obedience to God is a way to show love for Him.

— My child responds to the Lord through praise in word, song, and actions.

— My child appreciates creation, knowing that our heavenly Father is the Creator.

— My child understands that Bible characters made wise and foolish choices and that making wise choices is a way of showing love to the Lord.

— When praying, my child expresses love for God.

— My child understands that obeying parents is a way to show love for the Lord.

— My child enjoys learning about the Bible because the Bible is God's message to us.

— My child sits quietly and respectfully during prayer.

— My child values the Bible as the best way to know God.

(Others:)

—

—

Service Activities

___ My child serves by being obedient to his or her parents.

___ My child serves by obeying others in authority (teachers, babysitters, etc.).

___ My child sits quietly and respectfully in church.

___ My child enjoys memorizing verses and sharing them with others.

___ My child is a willing participant in classes at church.

___ My child enjoys doing age-appropriate service projects.

___ My child often tells others (friends, siblings) what he or she has learned.

___ My child shows kindness to others.

___ My child shows an attitude of thankfulness to others.

___ My child helps his or her parents in serving others.

(Others:)

___

___

THE FAMILY ITINERARY FOR FAMILIES WITH A KINDERGARTEN TO SECOND GRADER

Make this plan fit *your* family. Complete it at the beginning of each year while your child is in the early elementary stage. While keeping a focus throughout this time on acquiring Bible knowledge as a basis for life-living wisdom, each year you should study different verses, biographies, and aspects of this. Also review what you learned in previous years.

Our spiritual goals for the year are:

1.

2.

3.

4.

5.

6.

Our family verse for this year is:

We'll also study the following six additional verses (one every two months) about God and His character:

    1.

    2.

    3.

    4.

    5.

    6.

We'll also study the following six Bible biographies (one every two months):

    1.

    2.

    3.

    4.

    5.

    6.

We will also do a research study on this person in the Bible:

Choose someone from the Bible to look at more closely than you do in the biographies above. To feature what you learn about the character, design a scale model, write a play, record a DVD, construct a game, etc.

Here are other activities our family will do together to learn about Bible characters:

1.

2.

3.

4.

5.

6.

Here are some themes for family fun nights we would like to do this year:

1.

2.

3.

4.

5.

6.

These could include a field trip, vacation, craft project, etc.

Our family has completed this year's family itinerary and met our spiritual goals.

(Have each family member sign.)

PARTNERING WITH YOUR CHURCH

Be sure to look also at chapter 11 in part 2 of this book for ideas of how your church can partner with you in the early elementary years of your child's life.

Notice especially the information there about a "milestone celebration." This is a time to honor those families that have reached the goals in their family itinerary.

If your family is participating in a program that supports families in the spiritual nurturing of their children, you and your child may be presented a certificate for reaching this milestone. Also, a prayer partner/encourager/mentor may be assigned to your child or family. This person is asked to pray for and encourage your child as he or she grows into adulthood.

If your church doesn't have such a program, you can still adopt an older person in the church as a "grandma" or "grandpa" to encourage and pray for your child. Ask that person to pray for your family, and include him or her in an occasional family activity.

CHAPTER 4

OLDER ELEMENTARY
(AGES 8–11: THIRD THROUGH SIXTH GRADES)

MASTER LIFE THREAD: GRACE (GENESIS 41:51–52)

> *For the grace of God that brings salvation has appeared to all men. It*
> *teaches us to say "No" to ungodliness and worldly passions, and to live*
> *self-controlled, upright and godly lives in this present age.*
>
> TITUS 2:11–12

Scott adjusted his guitar as he sat down on a stool, then chuckled as he looked out over the congregation.

"I almost didn't get here today," he began. Then he told about his wild ride to church. With four children, getting everyone ready for church and in the van was always chaotic for Scott and his wife, but today they seemed to be running further behind than usual. As the minutes ticked by, Scott became more and more anxious, knowing he was scheduled to play a solo at the beginning of the service.

Finally the family was in the van and heading down the highway.

"Whatcha playing this morning?" his nine-year-old asked.

Scott explained that the song focused on grace—getting something we don't deserve. "God sent His Son to die for sinful humanity," he continued, as he turned the corner onto the main road. "He did it because He loves us, not because we deserve to be rescued from our sin. Our responsibility as Christians is to show God's grace to others in the way we live."

His son mulled this over and continued to ask questions.

Scott pulled up to an intersection as the light turned red. He waited patiently, then realized that the light wasn't about to turn green anytime soon. The regular traffic pattern had been interrupted because a train was coming down the tracks on the other side of the intersection. But Scott didn't need to go across the intersection; he only needed to turn left.

The train was one of those long, slow freight trains, and now Scott began to panic. He had ten minutes to get to church, and he needed every single one of those precious seconds. Waiting for a train wasn't an option if he planned to get there on time.

He looked around. No one else was out on this early Sunday morning. He made the choice to make a left turn on a red light.

Immediately a siren blared, and a flashing light appeared behind him. Too late, Scott realized someone else was up and about—a police officer.

Despondently, Scott pulled over.

"Officer," he begged, "I admit I'm in a hurry. I have to play at church at eleven o'clock. I understand about red lights, I really do, but I don't have time to wait for that train."

The officer looked at Scott and at his family, dressed in their Sunday best, now quiet and waiting—and watching.

"Okay," he said, "but don't do it again."

Scott pulled away and headed down the road.

"That," he said to his son, "was grace in action."

For your older elementary child, life is changing. He still enjoys learning, but the learning is expanding to include information a parent can't always control. He has more access to good things like art classes, libraries, and soccer games; but he also has more awareness of the bad things, such as drugs, crime, and abortion. You can no longer get by with vague answers when your child asks what that Planned Parenthood sign means, or why Susie's dad is in jail, or why the soldier who lives next door is going to a faraway place for a year. Life can become frightening without a parent's concerned and nurturing presence.

But God's grace, the very grace that draws your child to Christ, can also sustain your child through daily life. Dr. Tim Kimmel writes about grace in his book *Grace-Based Parenting:*

> Grace is what attracts us to Him and what confirms His love for us over and over. God's grace has the power to transform the most hardened, indifferent soul into a person spilling over with kindness. If God our heavenly Father is the perfect Father, and the primary way He deals with us as humans is through the power of His grace, it stands to reason that grace forms the best template for bringing out the best in our children. (Nashville: W Publishing, 2004, p. 28)

We're saved by grace. If your child has trusted Christ, he may not be able to eloquently define what he's done, but he understands he's a sinner in need of a Savior, and therefore he understands grace. In one sense, children may have a truer sense of their sinfulness than adults—because we parents are so quick to point out when children make bad choices. Yes, that's our responsibility, but sometimes we get carried away.

Children get scolded when they do something wrong, but, as an adult, I don't remember recently having to sit in time-out for gossiping. Nor have I ever been refused dessert for a bad attitude (though that might not be a bad idea). Nor have I ever been grounded for getting angry. As adults, we can easily overlook our faults until they no longer cause even a pinprick of conscience.

Children understand they're sinners and can possess a sensitive heart desire for the Savior. Because of His unlimited love, God provides that Savior in His Son, the Lord Jesus Christ. None of us is worthy of such a magnificent gift. Still, God offers it.

And grace expands beyond salvation.

Grace is what helps us feel comfort in God's love.

Grace is what enables us to make good life choices.

Grace is the essence of peace and security.

Grace is what causes us to respond to others with kindness.

Unlike most gifts, the gift of grace isn't a one-time in-the-moment gift, but one that continues day after day until the *end* of forever, one that's abundantly given to us by a loving God, and one that we need to reflect in how we respond to the minutiae of everyday life.

The gift of grace provides the following:

The basis for salvation. "[God] made us alive with Christ even when we were dead in transgressions—it is by grace you have been saved" (Ephesians 2:5).

Forgiveness of sins. "In him we have redemption through his blood, the forgiveness of sins, in accordance with the riches of God's grace" (Ephesians 1:7).

Direction for our Christian life. "Let your conversation be always full of grace, seasoned with salt, so that you may know how to answer everyone" (Colossians 4:6).

Reason for eternal encouragement and good hope. "May our Lord Jesus Christ himself and God our Father, who loved us and by his grace gave us eternal encouragement and good hope, encourage your hearts and strengthen you in every good deed and word" (2 Thessalonians 2:16–17).

Instruction for making right choices. "It teaches us to say 'No' to ungodliness and worldly passions, and to live self-controlled, upright and godly lives in this present age" (Titus 2:12).

As our children face the world with newfound independence, they need to understand all that God has done for them. This understanding transforms into a heart response to God's grace as revealed in the person and work of Christ.

Our children also need to understand mercy, since mercy is a primary aspect of grace. Understanding mercy is essential in recognizing God's response to us and our response to others. *Nelson's Illustrated Bible Dictionary* defines mercy as "the aspect of God's love that causes Him to help the miserable, just as grace is the aspect of His love that moves Him to forgive the guilty."

Like Scott, the friend I talked about at the beginning of this chapter, we need to look for opportunities to teach our children what grace is all about (though I don't recommend running a red light to do it).

Helping our children understand and respond in awe to God's priceless gift of grace will enable them to grow into adults who reflect Christ in the many nuances of life. God shows mercy and grace in His relationship to us; we need to show mercy and grace in our relationships with others.

WHAT THEY'RE LIKE:
CHARACTERISTICS OF THIRD TO SIXTH GRADERS

Children in this age-group continue to be rapid learners—although maybe you're not always happy with what your third to sixth grader is learning. She's learning both the good and the bad about life. As much as we'd like to think we do, we can no longer control everything she hears and sees. Even when we monitor computer and television use, the kids next door are unmonitored, and they're anxious to share what they've seen or heard.

We can try to isolate our children from the world, but unfortunately we can't isolate them from sin. Each child has a sin nature, and each child sins. Wise parents guide their children in developing the skills they'll need to live a godly life of integrity and courage even when that integrity and courage mean taking a solitary stand.

But there's another side to the third to sixth grader. These children have sensitive hearts. Faith becomes very personal to them. Many of them respond to Christ during these years, and many make the decision to become pastors or missionaries or to serve God in other ways. Often these decisions are defining moments in their lives.

My own husband trusted Christ as an eleven-year-old at church camp. As his counselor (a missionary) talked to him, he said, "You don't have to go to another country to serve the Lord. You could be a pastor or a—"

"That's what I'll be," Ken said. "I'll be a pastor." He never wavered from that decision made as an eleven-year-old. As an adult, he had a burden for ministering to children and encouraging them to serve the Lord. He understood the seriousness of the decision he made as a kid.

How do we parent these children and recognize their vulnerabilities?

Here are ten characteristics of this age-group that can aid in the learning process.

1. *They like to go places and do things.* As parents we can give them opportunity to try new things, to develop new interests, and to see new places—all the while guiding them in right directions. Get excited about life and all the different places to go and things to do. (Computers are fun, but there's more to life than staring at a screen.) Remind your children that God, in His grace, gave us a big, wonderful world to enjoy.

Appreciate what God has done for us, and don't allow your children to be bored. (As the saying goes, life is boring only to boring people.) As a kid, I wasn't allowed to say I was bored. If I did, I knew my dad would find something for me to do—like clean the garage. That kept me fairly happily doing anything else. My husband and I had the same rule in our house, and it worked on our kids too.

God, in His grace, has provided so much for us. We need to teach our kids to actively appreciate what He's done.

2. *They want proof.* This desire for proof shows up on age-characteristic charts. It was also evident in our Biggest Question Survey. Older elementary–age children no longer believe something *only* because an adult said it (although they do still believe parents *most* of the time). What a challenging but exciting responsibility to answer their questions and teach them *why* we believe the Bible.

Of course, the key to believing the Bible is faith. And the more your children know about the Bible, the more difficult it will be for someone to shake their faith.

Don't forget external Bible evidence. Sometimes this is an area we often neglect, yet many children this age are seriously interested in subjects such as archaeology, and they enjoy learning facts about ancient manuscripts and recent archaeological findings.

3. *They're hero-worshippers.* Have you had an argument with your son because you won't let him hang an inappropriate celebrity poster in his room? Have you had arguments with your daughter about what magazines she reads? Have you been to a teenager clothing store and looked at the immodest, celebrity-look-alike clothing that your daughter "must" have?

I remember asking a group of middle school students (just one notch above elementary school age) about their heroes. The answers were astounding as kids listed celebrities with blatantly bad lifestyles. Encourage your children to emulate Bible characters, Christian musicians, Christian athletes, or even a high school or college kid in your church who's living a godly life.

And don't despair. Many children this age say their parents are their heroes. What better heroes could they have?

4. *They desire justice.* They want to know if something's right or if it's wrong and don't want to hear some speech about middle ground. When listening to a group of third to sixth graders at play, you often hear the cry, "That's *not fair!*"

This is a hard lesson we must teach our kids: Life often *isn't* fair. Sometimes very bad things happen to very good people. Sin messed up our world. Instead of living in a perfect garden, we live in a world with tornadoes, hurricanes, fires, crime, hatred, racism, and other tragedies.

But God *is* just (Isaiah 30:18). He's also sovereign, and nothing that happens in our sin-filled world surprises Him. He's a sovereign God with a sovereign plan.

5. *They enjoy planning and building.* How-to books (about the right subjects) are big hits with third to sixth graders. They want to know how to do things—whether it's building a tree house or braiding hair. Use this desire as a teaching tool. For instance, you could suggest they build a scale model of the tabernacle or the marketplace in Nazareth. Or have them plan a family service project.

6. *They enjoy reading.* Not every fifth grader will spend his leisure time reading a book, but many of them do. Take advantage of this love of reading by helping your child find appropriate adventures, mysteries, and how-to books. Get a set of missionary biographies (or check out child-appropriate DVDs about missionaries). These often combine adventure *and* good Bible truth. They can also be influential in the decisions your child makes about his own future.

7. *They understand that adults are fallible.* Younger children often think parents can do no wrong. But as our children move into the older elementary years, they begin to notice the flaws. They pay attention when you have an argument about unpaid bills or about how the scratch got on the car. They notice when you break a promise because you're busy watching the football game or e-mailing your sister. Children begin to understand that even the best parents fail.

In fact, sometimes outside circumstances cause us to break promises we truly want to keep: Car trouble keeps us from taking our son to the zoo; a case of the flu keeps us from attending the school band concert; a required late night at work keeps us from helping with homework. Children need to understand that parents don't have control over every circumstance.

But when we break promises because of our own choice, we need to admit it. Since breaking a promise can hurt a child in several ways, we need to carry through on what we say. When we break a promise, it doesn't justify disrespect on the part of the child—the parent still is in authority.

We, as parents, need to talk to our children about human fallibility. Only God can keep all promises. Only God never makes a mistake in relationship to His children. We can remind our children that God's promise keeping is another aspect of grace. Even when we don't deserve the fulfillment of a promise, God is faithful.

Remind your child how much you love her. And remember, children are very forgiving. Family members need to show grace to each other.

8. *They enjoy classifying information to reach a conclusion.* Teachers take advantage of this characteristic in school, and we should take advantage of it while teaching them the Bible. Allow them to put events along a timeline or to categorize which Bible characters showed trust in God and which didn't.

9. *They're more aware of those around them.* They're learning that others may have a different perspective on life than they do. They can become burdened for their friends who live in difficult situations. They may hurt for the child whose dad left home or the kid who everyone teases. They may pray daily for a child whose parents have an idol prominently displayed in the living room for family worship.

This is a great opportunity to encourage kids to show God's grace to those around them and to praise them for doing so.

10. *They enjoy friendships.* Friends are the people they do homework with, play with, laugh with, whine to, dress like, talk like, e-mail to, text to, and call on the phone. Friends are a huge part of their lives. Our responsibility is to teach our kids the biblical instructions on friendship (and there are a lot of them). We need to talk about the importance of sharing God's grace with friends.

WHAT THEY'RE ASKING:
QUESTIONS THIRD TO SIXTH GRADERS HAVE ABOUT GOD AND THE BIBLE

Kids in the third-to-sixth-grade age-group willingly and eagerly told us their biggest question about God and the Bible. Some had more than one question.

Their desire to know about the Bible's accuracy and trustworthiness was the biggest difference between this age-group and younger kids. Their questions showed they were thinking about what they'd been taught. Their quest for answers puts a lot of responsibility on us as parents and teachers. At the same time, we can see their questions as a sign of maturing faith. They need to know why they should believe what we've told them. They need to "own" their faith and not be dependent on their parents or church leadership.

Why not ask your child what his biggest question is about God and the Bible? You might be surprised. We can't always answer the questions they ask, but we can listen patiently and help them find the answers.

Here are top questions that were asked by third to sixth graders.

1. *How do we know the Bible is true?*

- Because the Bible is God's Word (John 17:17).
- Because people witnessed the events of the Bible (2 Peter 1:16).
- Because the Bible is historically correct (1 John 1:1–2).
- Because God used at least forty men to write the Bible—yet it all fits together (Luke 1:1–2; 4).
- Because the Bible was written over a time period of fifteen hundred years.
- Because events that were prophesied really happened (Jeremiah 28:9).

2. *Why did the Lord Jesus do amazing things like miracles?*

A miracle is something that can be done only by God's power. The miracles done by the Lord Jesus were proof that He had God's power—He was sent by God the Father to save people from their sins. He wanted them to know He is the Son of God, and doing miracles was one way He communicated this to them. Unfortunately, most people didn't believe. They liked the miracles, but they didn't like Jesus claiming to be the Son of God.

3. *Why did Adam and Eve's sin mess stuff up for everyone?*

Adam represented all people. When he sinned, all people became separated from God. When Christ—the "last Adam" (1 Corinthians 15:45)—came, He stayed righteous and died for our sins. Christ is also a representative for all people, and now when we trust Him as Savior, we're made righteous as well.

4. *How can God be three persons in one?*

This question is difficult—and one we can't completely answer. The Bible tells us that God the Father, God the Son (Jesus), and God the Holy Spirit are three distinct persons but all one God (Matthew 3:16–17).

Many parents and teachers use illustrations such as the three parts of an egg or an apple or the three roles someone might have (a wife, a mom, and a teacher). Although these illustrations can help, all human illustrations of the Trinity eventually break down.

The best answer to some questions is this: "I can't explain that. God is God, and He is different from us. He doesn't choose to tell us some things. But I believe what the Bible tells me, and this is what the Bible says."

5. *Why are there so many different kinds of Bibles?*

In different Bibles, the words for the same verse are sometimes different from one another. People have reworded verses with the goal of making them easier to understand. But the verses have the same meaning.

We've all heard the joke about the boy who asks his dad, "Where did I come from?" After the father stammers and stutters through an answer, the boy responds, "Oh, I thought I came from Pittsburgh."

In a way, this is the same type of question. Children don't need a lengthy answer about the distinctives and relative strengths of the various popular Bible translations. That's not what they're asking.

Often adults are the ones who create confusion in the minds of children. Our daughter reads a verse from her Bible, and we casually remark, "Oh, that's different from my Bible." Of course, we mean that the *words* are different, not the meaning, but a child could easily understand our statement to mean that Bibles have different books, thoughts, and concepts. We need to explain that there are many different versions, but the meaning is the same in all (as well as in Bibles written in other languages).

WHAT YOU CAN DO:
SUGGESTIONS FOR TEACHING YOUR THIRD TO SIXTH GRADER HOW TO APPLY GOD'S *GRACE* IN RELATIONSHIPS WITH OTHERS

What about Salvation?

Many adults look back to the third-to-sixth-grade years as the time when they truly understood salvation and made the decision to trust Christ.

You can't force your children to accept God's gift of grace; that's their own decision. But you can talk with them about the importance of becoming a Christian and make sure they understand the gospel message.

- Teach them from the Bible that salvation is God's grace-filled gift to us.
- Review the consequences of not trusting Christ.
- Share your own testimony—especially if this is around the age when you trusted Christ. Why are you glad that you made the decision to become a Christian? What difference does Christ make in your everyday life?
- Ask them questions. (Do this gently; it's not an inquisition.) Why don't they want to make a decision for Christ? Is there something about salvation they don't understand? Answer their questions with kindness and clarity.
- Expose them to the testimonies of others. Give them opportunities to meet other Christians—an athlete giving a testimony at a local sports clinic, a missionary you invite to your house for dinner, or counselors at a Christian camp.

Again, don't push. Sometimes kids react to pushiness by resisting what you're saying. Not understanding the serious nature of the decision, they react instead to the power of having control over a parent. As sad as this scenario is, it does happen.

When your child does trust Christ, tell him to write down the date, place, time, and circumstances on the inside cover of his Bible. This gives him a tangible date to remember if later he ever doubts his salvation.

Ideas and More Ideas …

Although not all these ideas focus solely on the life thread of grace, they're valuable activities for the spiritual nurturing of your child.

1. *Attend meetings that introduce dads and moms to your church's vision for supporting parents as you spiritually nurture your children.*

2. *Attend your church's meeting for parents where staff members and experienced parents give ideas for spiritually training older elementary–age children.* Time may be set aside during this meeting for you to complete your family itinerary for the year. If not, fill it out at home as soon as possible. In your itinerary, include regularly scheduled family nights when you participate in a family activity, have a short Bible lesson, and memorize a verse together. Or work on helping your child memorize verses he is already required to remember.

3. *Reconnect (if you've lost connection) with the person or couple assigned to pray for and encourage your family.* Thank them for their help. (See page 189 to read about the mentor/prayer partner suggestion.)

4. *Choose a family verse for the year.* Your child is now old enough to have a say in which verse to choose. In fact, you could allow him to choose the verse himself. Make sure you ask him to explain why he made that choice. If you have several children, allow them each to choose a verse for the family to learn.

5. *Join a small group, Sunday school class, or parenting class.* You'll be encouraged by talking with others who are traveling through the same stages of parenting you are. Encourage friendships between your children and the children of the parents in the class.

6. *Ask your child what she's learned at church.* Follow up with some questions: "Why is that Bible character important?" "What do you think you would have done if your were Noah [or Lydia, or Peter]?"

Reinforce the lessons by retelling them at home.

7. *Read any blogs, Web pages, or newsletters your church may have for parents or for older elementary*

children. Some churches are diligent about doing a blog or newsletter but have difficulty getting parents to actually read them. Take advantage of what your church offers.

8. *Discuss the grace and mercy of God.* Ask your child why we need to learn about the awesomeness and authority of God before we can understand God's grace and mercy. If your child struggles to come to a conclusion, guide her thinking. We need to understand the magnificence, power, sovereignty, and righteousness of God before we can understand the ultimate sacrifice of grace and mercy for us. We are unworthy and unrighteous people, but God loves us (Romans 5:17).

9. *Balance schedules.* Children this age begin to get busy with school, sports, and friends. Sometimes we allow them to put everything else before the Lord. Soccer practice comes before Sunday morning church. (Soccer is *only* for six weeks.) Drama classes come before Scripture memorization. (Well, she can't memorize *everything.*) Friends come before family. (Shana is at her friend's house again? I thought we were having a family night.)

Obviously, these activities are good and important in a child's life—but when we cancel out church for sports, or agree that our child's life is too busy for Scripture memory, or neglect Christ-centered family times, we're sending a message. We might not be verbally communicating it, but we're showing our child that the Lord is last on the life-priority list. We need to find a balance.

As our child asks to be in this or that activity, we need to set nonnegotiables. We need to balance out the different areas of a child's life.

10. *Challenge your child to look up any words she doesn't understand while reading the Bible.* Sometimes we think (adults as well as kids) that to understand a difficult word in a verse, we need to be theologians with a library of commentaries. Not true. Most words can be understood with a quick lookup in a regular dictionary.

11. *Teach your child how to use a Bible dictionary and concordance.* Yes, your child can get a definition from a regular dictionary, but by the time he's in fifth or sixth grade, he should also be able to use a Bible encyclopedia, word-study reference book, and concordance. Even many Hebrew/Greek dictionaries and word studies are basic enough for a kid to use—especially if you're there beside him, giving guidance.

Invest in a Bible software program and teach your fifth or sixth grader how to use it. (They aren't difficult. In fact, your kids will probably soon be teaching you how to use it!) Bible software programs can provide a lot of information quickly, as most include everything from concordances and topical studies to maps and photos.

12. *Recognize that children in this age-group are hero-worshippers.* Do a study on David. Talk about his strength, his good looks, his intelligence—and how the crowds cheered for him (1 Samuel 18:6–7). Assign your child to make a poster about David—as if he were coming to your church or civic auditorium for a concert. Do a study on the servant of Naaman's wife (2 Kings). Why do we know she was an obedient servant? How did God use her? Teach your child that these people were real people with real problems—and great heroes for the Lord.

13. *Ask your pastor and his family over to dinner.* Give your child the opportunity to get to know him. (My husband loved getting to know the children in our church. He kidded around with them, gave them nicknames, and was available and eager to answer their questions. "Kids aren't the church of tomorrow," he would say. "They're the church of today.")

14. *Teach your children from the church doctrinal statement.* Be creative. Study one point per month. Many of these are basic truths from the Bible that your children may already know. But by getting them familiar with the doctrinal statement, you're showing that your church has a set of nonnegotiable, biblically based beliefs and that people who serve in the church must agree to them. (In one church, a man began attending who held some perverse doctrine. He charmed his way past the board and became a member—then started teaching nonbiblical doctrine in a high school Sunday school class. The teenagers themselves caught it and went to the board. I give a lot of credit to that church for training its kids well enough to quickly perceive something was wrong. A lot of teenagers would have simply "taken it in.")

15. *Teach your children the meaning of the church ordinances.* Your children may already understand Communion and baptism. If they don't, now's the time to make sure they do. If your church has classes to help them understand, allow your children to attend. Even if parents aren't specifically involved, sit in the class or ask for an outline so you can back up what was taught.

16. *Seek out good heroes and heroines for your children.* If your child is a baseball fan and a collegiate or professional player who's a Christian is speaking at a church or convention center, take your child to the event. Be willing to stand in line for an autograph. When my brother was in fifth grade, Phil Regan, a Chicago Cubs pitcher, attended our church. Phil had a great testimony *and* a son the same age as Roger. Once, Roger was invited to attend a Cubs game with the Regan family. Now, grown with kids of his own, Roger still remembers the thrill of going to a game with a player. Do what you can to make those kinds of memories.

17. *Read books together.* Choose books about people who have done something heroic or have taken a stand when everyone else was doing wrong. Make the book-sharing time fun with popcorn and hot

chocolate or pizza and soda. Read books about people such as John Newton (who wrote the hymn "Amazing Grace"), Adoniram Judson, James Irwin, or Amy Carmichael. Some Christian publishers have series of biographical books for children.

18. *Do a project with your child.* Some examples:

Photography—Take pictures that show the awesomeness of God.

Art—Challenge him to do a painting of a Bible character you've studied together.

Media—Make a DVD telling the story of someone doing a service project.

Building—Design the plans for the optimal church (using Legos or other construction-type blocks).

Sewing/knitting—Make mittens, scarves, bibs, etc., for a local mission.

19. *Go on a family missions trip.* Many churches have family missions trips where parents and kids go somewhere to help out a missionary or Christian organization. Third to sixth graders can be a big help. They can carry water and food to the workers, clean up material scraps, entertain younger children (often a big help for working parents), run errands, etc. Make sure you appreciate them and acknowledge their value in completing the task. Begin a tradition of service that may last a lifetime.

20. *Visit Christian organizations in your area.* Maybe you can't afford to go on a missions trip or one isn't available. You can still reach out to others by offering to serve at Christian organizations in your area. (Check out homeless shelters, rescue missions, or nursing homes.) You and your child can stuff envelopes, hang posters of an upcoming event around town, or set tables for a fund-raising banquet. Encourage them to have a good attitude as they serve with grace.

Discuss the seriousness of the service; at the same time, make the day fun (not burdensome). Start with breakfast at a favorite restaurant. Pray that the Lord will use your family. Keep a scrapbook dedicated to family service projects, including highlights of the day and pictures. Periodically look over the scrapbook, and pray for the people whom you've met.

21. *Challenge your older children to help the younger children.* Ask your older child to choose a Bible character from the preschool or early elementary list of biographies. Encourage her to do some further study on the character and then do a puppet show, skit, or other presentation of the character for younger siblings. She could do this on a family night. Tell her to include how the biography shows God's grace or the person's grace toward others.

22. *Listen to your children.* Many third to sixth graders enjoy talking—and enjoy it a *lot*. I remember my daughter coming home from school and giving me daily updates on just about everyone in her class.

These kids can ramble on for hours, chatting about who failed the geography test, who got a new dog, who has a birthday coming, what so-and-so was wearing, and who threw up all over the teacher's shoes. You name it, many kids this age can talk about it. Are all these childish news reports really important?

Yes, you may quickly get tired of their chatter and want them to be quiet. But here's something parents of children in this age-group need to know: A few years from now, you'll be begging them to talk with you. If you don't patiently listen to them when they're ten, they won't be talking to you when they're thirteen or fourteen or fifteen—ages when you would do most anything to find out what's happening in their lives.

This is how we show grace to our kids. We listen. We take interest. We ask the next day: "Is Emma doing better in geography? What did Michael name his dog? What does Annie want for her birthday? What did Lauren wear today? Is Carsten feeling better?"

You'll reap the benefits of being a patient listener. Your child instinctively knows: "Dad listened to me when I was telling him all that silly stuff. He'll listen to me now that I need to talk to him about something important."

Our heavenly Father patiently listens to us go on and on. We need to show that same understanding and grace to our kids.

23. *Teach self-control.* We're saved by grace, and we live by grace. Titus tells us that grace is our teacher—teaching us to turn away from ungodliness and live self-controlled lives. The later elementary years can be tough ones. Kids are exposed to more and more of the world around them and learning more and more things you wish they wouldn't learn.

We need to teach them balance. (Six hours of daily TV watching or computer games isn't balanced.) Ten minutes a day in memory work will result in many well-learned verses. A half hour of piano or guitar practice will enable them to become good musicians. Backing away from an aggravating situation with a younger brother instead of throwing your flip-flops at him will result in a better outcome.

Is your child struggling with temptation? Maybe your child has picked up some inappropriate language, or wants to give up in math, or eats too much junk food. We need to encourage her to come to us for help. If we ignore her problem, we send a message of wrong priorities and values. We're the parents and we need to help. What better way for a kid to find a solution to a problem than to talk it out with a loving, concerned parent offering counsel on God's Word?

24. *Study spiritual gifts with your child.* Do a study on the spiritual gifts (as in Romans 12) and what gifts your child is beginning to demonstrate. Even at this age (and younger) some children lean

toward one gift or another. Talk about ways your child can use his gifts in church, school, or the neighborhood.

Don't stop with the spiritual gift verses in Romans 12. The entire chapter has great verses for Christian living.

25. *Adapt familiar games to review Bible knowledge.* For instance, you could play charades of Bible events, a true-or-false quiz game, or twenty questions (about a Bible person, place, or event). Encourage your child's creativity, and have him come up with his own game. Although some games may be too difficult for a younger child, include your preschoolers and children in early elementary grades when possible.

26. *Adopt a family or make a new friend.* Encourage your child to show grace to others by inviting them to your house for dinner or other family activities or by visiting them and helping out in their homes (raking leaves, shoveling snow, mowing the lawn).

Do this for a new-to-the-neighborhood family, a lonely person, a shut-in, a refugee family your church has sponsored, an international student attending a nearby university, a single parent who's struggling (especially if he or she has a child the same age as yours), or an older person without family or whose family lives far away. (Older people who are homebound can get especially lonely.)

Talk with your children about what you can do to make the person feel loved and appreciated. Children are great at coming up with ideas—some you probably haven't thought about. Do something for the person or family you "adopt" at least once a month.

27. *Encourage your child to write a psalm.* Have her divide her song into three parts: (1) knowing God, (2) loving God, (3) serving God.

Does your child play the piano, guitar, or other instrument? Challenge her to write music for the words.

28. *Celebrate spiritual birthdays.* This doesn't need to be a big celebration, but rather a reminder of the decision the child (or adult) made on that particular day to trust Christ as Savior. Some parents buy special gifts for their children: a picture (with a Scripture verse) to hang on the wall, a Bible, a devotional book, or a Bible cover. Cook the child's favorite meal, or take her out to her favorite restaurant. By your actions, you're letting her know the day is important.

29. *Start family traditions.* With your child's help, create a family tradition.

The women and girls in my extended family celebrate Purim (thanks to the creativity of my daughter's mother-in-law). Each spring we get together for a Saturday brunch and celebrate bold, brave, beautiful women who trusted God and did what was right. Before the day, we each choose a "bold, brave, beautiful woman" to research. We write up a short bio of the woman and make copies for each of the other women. After we eat, we read the story of Esther (to the little girls) from a small book that my daughter's mother-in-law wrote and illustrated. Then we take turns sharing about the women we've researched. We collect copies of all the biographies and keep them in our individual notebooks. Then we toast each other with pickles, honoring all bold, brave, beautiful women who trust God and do what's right. Our Purim celebration has included great-grandmas and babies.

We've been doing this for several years. Bios have included Abigail (in the Bible), Sarah Polk, Fanny Crosby, and Gladys Aylward.

You can borrow our tradition or make your own.

30. *Talk to your child about the importance of sharing her faith with other people.* If you have unsaved relatives whom your child sees on a regular basis, discuss ways you can show love and grace to those people. In such situations, actions are often louder than words. Tell her that Grandpa is watching the way your immediate family lives, reacts to difficult situations, and shows kindness to others. Sometimes children can break through a tough-shelled person in a way that adults can't. As a family, pray for Grandpa before each visit.

BIOS AND VERSES:
SUGGESTED BIBLE VERSES AND BIOGRAPHIES TO TEACH YOUR THIRD TO SIXTH GRADER

For looking closer at Bible characters and for memorizing verses, here are suggestions to get you started as you chart your family itinerary toward the life thread of understanding God's grace and reflecting that grace in your relationships with others.

You may want to coordinate these discovery topics and memory verses with what the church is focusing on in its teaching ministry to your child's age-group.

Biographies

1. *Noah* in Genesis 6:9—9:19. Review the story of Noah—this time emphasizing the wickedness

of the people and the trust of Noah. Because of his trust, "Noah found favor in the eyes of the LORD" (Genesis 6:8).

2. *Joseph* in Genesis 37—50. Review his story, emphasizing his grace toward his brothers when they came to him for grain. They sold him as a slave; he could have refused to help them.

3. *David* in 1 Samuel 24:8. David here is getting too much honor, and Saul no longer likes him. In fact, Saul hates him and takes his men out to the hills in search of the fleeing David. David, in turn, gets close enough to Saul to cut off part of his robe. He could've easily killed Saul but, instead, showed him grace. "You are more righteous than I," Saul later responded. "You have treated me well, but I have treated you badly" (1 Samuel 24:17).

4. *David* in 2 Samuel 9:6–13. David again shows grace and mercy, this time to Jonathan's son Mephibosheth, who as a five-year-old had lost the use of his legs when his nurse dropped him. Now he's an adult, useless because of his injuries. David sought him out and gave him his grandfather Saul's property. David also invited him to sit at the king's table. This is a beautiful picture of the grace and mercy God gives to us.

5. *Naaman's servant girl* in 2 Kings 5:1–27. She made a difference in the life of a VIP. She was taken from her home and forced to become a slave. I think she must've done her job well and obediently; if the slave girl wasn't trustworthy, Naaman's wife wouldn't have listened to her when she talked about Elisha. Naaman's leprosy was cured, and he realized that the God of Israel was the one true God.

6. *Jesus* in Matthew 2; Luke 2. Our children know the events of Christ's birth, and most can repeat them backward and forward. Don't allow your children to become apathetic about it. The Lord Jesus Christ is God's great gift to us. Each year have a family goal of discovering something new about these chapters. Why were the shepherds so close to Bethlehem? (They were raising sheep for the temple sacrifices.) How many wise men were there? (Probably an entire caravan—people didn't travel in small groups. The tradition is three because there were three gifts.)

My boss's family memorized Luke 2:1–20 with their kids, building on their tradition of acting out the story. Now they can quote it as they role-play the action.

7. *The good Samaritan* in Luke 10:30–36. (This of course is a parable, not a true biography about a real person.) This is a story Jesus told about grace, mercy, and kindness. The Samaritan was willing to help the hurting man and do what he could to make sure he had what he needed.

8. *The prodigal son* in Luke 15:1–23. (This, too, is a parable Jesus told.) This young man took his

father's money and ran away. Then he wasted the money and ended up living with pigs! His father welcomed him home with great love. What a beautiful picture of grace and mercy!

9. *Jesus* in John 19—21. Christ's death and resurrection are something children need to know. Yes, these chapters are harsh. We can shelter our children from the violence, or we can explain the price the Lord Jesus Christ had to pay for our salvation. He died for each one of us. Children this age are sensitive and will take this narrative personally and seriously—as they should. Christ died because of His love and grace toward us.

10. *Philemon* in Paul's letter to Philemon. This isn't someone we hear about much, but he's a great example of grace in relationship to others. His slave Onesimus did something wrong (perhaps he stole valuables from Philemon's house) and then escaped. Paul met Onesimus and shared the message of salvation. The slave trusted Christ, and Paul sent him back to Philemon with a letter. Culturally, Philemon had the right to kill Onesimus, but Paul encouraged him to accept him as a brother in Christ. (Although the Bible doesn't tell us that Philemon forgave him, the assumption is that he did. Paul knew Philemon well enough to understand his capacity for forgiveness.) "No longer as a slave, but better than a slave, as a dear brother. He is very dear to me but even dearer to you, both as a man and as a brother in the Lord" (Philemon v. 16).

Memory Verses

Proverbs 3:5–6. Children this age begin questioning the whys and hows behind the truths they've been taught. We can give them external evidences that the Bible is true, but they need to trust in God. They need faith. Without faith, the external evidence means nothing. With faith, they can lean on the Lord, recognizing His sovereignty and control.

Isaiah 9:6. Isaiah wrote about the coming Savior, an event that wouldn't happen for another seven centuries. Because of God's love and grace, He designed a plan of redemption for sinful humanity.

This verse describes the character of Christ: Wonderful Counselor, Mighty God, Everlasting Father, Prince of Peace. Teach these characteristics to children by using hand motions. (Some children may feel they're too old for motions. That's okay. Even going through them once may help them remember the words. Or you could have your older kids teach the motions to their younger siblings.)

Wonderful Counselor—place hand behind ear as if listening

Mighty God—arm curled to show muscle (for mighty)

Everlasting Father—crossing hands over chest to show love

Prince of Peace—hands on head forming a crown

Compare this verse to Luke 2 as an example of fulfilled prophecy that children can easily understand. Fulfilled prophecy is evidence that the Bible's true.

Isaiah 44:6. A verse reminding children to respect the awesomeness and authority of God. God is all-powerful. No other god is like Him. He's the beginning and the end.

John 1:14. The Lord Jesus Christ is the personification of grace and truth. We can't separate grace and truth from His character. His act of grace (dying for us) is the greatest sacrifice someone could make for a friend. (See also John 15:13.)

Romans 12:1–2. As children begin to understand God's grace, they should also understand their responsibility to reach out to others with grace. Here Paul writes that we're to give our very selves as a sacrifice to the service of God.

1 Corinthians 10:13. Peer pressure is all around. Children this age like to be liked, and they have a tendency to follow what others are doing. Children need to be confident in saying no when pressured to make wrong choices, but they also need to learn the importance of treating others with graciousness (rather than argumentatively or judgmentally).

2 Corinthians 5:17. Because of God's grace, we're offered new life in the Lord Jesus Christ. Our responsibility is to share that message with others, not only by our words, but also by our behavior.

Philippians 2:9–10. A good reminder of the awesomeness and authority of God.

Ephesians 2:4–5. God has so much love. He looks on us poor, struggling sinners and shows us mercy. Because of His grace, He saved us. Because of His grace, we have the ability to help others.

Titus 2:11–13. We're saved by grace, and grace is our teacher. Because of God's grace, we have knowledge and ability to live our daily lives according to His will.

WHAT NOT TO DO:
COMMON ERRORS TO AVOID WITH THIRD TO SIXTH GRADERS

I've been both a pastor's kid and a pastor's wife, and I've been involved in a lot of children's and youth ministries. Unfortunately, I've talked to a lot of kids (and adults) who didn't want anything to do with the Lord. I've heard a lot of rationale, but one cause pops up again and again. We saw it on the Biggest Question Survey, and unbelievably, I recently heard a pastor say it from his pulpit.

It's this: "God's not listening to me. He doesn't answer my prayers anymore; why should I listen to Him?"

In my opinion, one of the biggest disservices we fall into is that of confusing answered prayer with getting what we want. Of course, we tell kids, "God doesn't always answer yes." But that's not what we communicate.

Take this scenario.

On Sunday morning, Pastor Joe asks his children's class, "Do you have any prayer requests?"

Maggie wants prayer for her aunt's sore toe.

Dylan wants prayer for his family's safe trip to visit relatives in Pittsburgh.

LeAnn wants prayer for a new puppy.

Everyone prays.

The next week they return. Pastor Joe says, "Has anyone had any answered prayer this week?"

Maggie excitedly raises her hand because her aunt's sore toe is better. Pastor Joe is excited and writes that down on the whiteboard under "Answered Prayer."

Dylan and his family went to Pittsburgh and back. "Oh, another answered prayer," says Pastor Joe. He dutifully adds it to the Answered Prayer list.

But poor LeAnn didn't get a puppy. Pastor Joe says they'll wait and see if God answers her prayer the next week.

But LeAnn's prayer *was* answered. She talked to her parents, and they said the family absolutely could *not* get a puppy because of her dad's allergies. Yet because LeAnn didn't get what she wanted, Pastor Joe unknowingly communicates that her prayer wasn't answered.

We teach children that prayer is more of a Christmas list than a talk with their heavenly Father. Sooner or later, the child won't get what he wants and prays for. Aunt June will die. Dad will lose his job. Mom will be in a car accident. And the child is devastated because "God didn't hear my prayers."

Yes, we're to make our requests known unto God. In Philippians 4:6, Paul wrote: "Do not be anxious about anything, but in everything, by prayer and petition, with thanksgiving, present your requests to God." Prayer is aligning ourselves to God's will, with thanksgiving: "Lord, if I get a puppy or I don't get a puppy, I'll be thankful."

And God does listen. He doesn't promise that everything will always go exactly the way we want it to go. We live in a messed-up world with tornadoes and cancer and unemployment. But even during the bad times, God is still with us, helping us through those situations and willingly offering peace that goes beyond any peace that the world could give us.

As we pray our requests with persistence and thanksgiving, God promises peace that goes above and beyond anything we can even understand: "And the peace of God, which transcends all understanding, will guard your hearts and your minds in Christ Jesus" (Philippians 4:7).

Sometimes we teach our children to focus their prayers on things. Instead we should be teaching them to pray for an attitude of thankfulness, for wisdom, for hearts of love and service, and for courage to make right choices.

Sometimes we get what we ask; sometimes we don't. But no matter what, God is listening. He loves us. He cares. He knows what's best. That's what we need to convey to our kids.

CHECKLIST FOR PARENTS OF THIRD TO SIXTH GRADERS

Time for a checkup. Remember, this checklist is for all four years from third through sixth grade, and a sixth grader would know more than a third grader (we hope).

Not all these statements will fit all children. This checklist is a guide for you, the parent, to evaluate whether you need to emphasize a particular area in your child's spiritual growth. Use the checklist to gauge what areas you may have missed, so you can review those areas with your child. And use the blank lines to add your own areas to review.

Again, this list is a guide—not a test.

Knowledge Commitments

___ My child remembers the truths learned as a preschooler about the awesomeness and authority of God. *(Use the preschool checklist as a guide.)*

___ My child remembers truths learned in the early elementary years about God and the Bible. *(Use the early elementary checklist as a guide.)*

___ My child knows how to explain the gospel message.

___ My child knows the definitions of grace and mercy.

___ My child knows the Bible biographies of people who demonstrated grace in their lives.

___ My child knows why people say Bibles are different from one another.

___ My child has a basic understanding of the spiritual gifts.

___ My child has an overall understanding of our church doctrine, ordinances, and organization. *(Ask your child questions about basic beliefs studied while learning about your church doctrine.)*

___ My child has a beginning understanding of biblical apologetics.

___ My child knows the importance of telling others about the gospel.

(Others:)

—

—

Love Indicators

___ My child is thankful to be saved by God's grace.

___ My child displays trust, reverence, and respect for God.

___ My child expresses awe and gratitude for God's creation and attributes.

___ My child is gaining confidence in Bible skills and enjoys reading and learning about our heavenly Father.

___ My child knows that the Bible is true, and my child steadfastly trusts what it says.

___ My child shows guilt and remorse for sin.

___ My child understands the forgiveness of God.

___ My child obeys me and other authorities willingly.

___ My child desires to know God better through Bible study and prayer.

___ My child extends grace and forgiveness to others even when they don't deserve it.

(Others:)

—

—

Service Activities

__ My child participates in church services with respectful behavior.

__ My child is welcoming to new kids at church and willing to help them get acclimated.

__ My child is quick to respond spontaneously when someone's in need of assistance.

__ My child is sensitive to those who are needy.

__ My child knows some missionaries personally and is interested in their service.

__ My child willingly takes part in family service projects.

__ My child regularly prays for others.

__ My child is interested in learning more about the Bible.

__ My child shares the gospel with others.

__ My child willingly helps out around the house and understands the importance of a family working together.

(Others:)

__

__

THE FAMILY ITINERARY FOR FAMILIES WITH A THIRD TO SIXTH GRADER

This plan should reflect the age of your child. At this age, he can begin taking part in helping you plan what to do.

Make this plan fit *your* family as you complete it at the beginning of each year while your child is in the older elementary stage. While keeping a focus throughout this time on the grace of God, you can study different verses, biographies, and aspects of God's grace each year.

This form is a worksheet. After you get your plan in place, you may want to put it on your computer or have your child make an artistic poster of your plan to hang on your wall.

Our spiritual goals for the year are:

1.

2.

3.

4.

5.

6.

Our family verse for this year is:

We'll also study the following six additional verses (one every two months) about God's grace:

    1.

    2.

    3.

    4.

    5.

    6.

We'll also study the following six Bible biographies (one every two months):

    1.

    2.

    3.

    4.

    5.

    6.

We'll do the following family service project to reach out to people in need:

(This could be "adopting" a single-parent family at church, cheering up nursing home residents, or going on a missions trip.)

My child's spiritual gift is:

(You might not know this for sure, but children often show personality traits or interests that reflect a particular God-given gift.)

Here's how my child uses that gift:

Four special family nights we plan to do this year are:

1.

2.

3.

4.

Our family has completed this year's family itinerary and met our spiritual goals.

(Have each family member sign.)

PARTNERING WITH YOUR CHURCH

Be sure to look also at chapter 12 in part 2 of this book for ideas of how your church can partner with you in the older elementary years of your child's life.

Notice especially the information there about a "milestone celebration." This is a time to honor those families that have reached their goals in their family itinerary.

If your family is participating in a program that supports families in the spiritual nurturing of their children, you and your child may be presented with a certificate of completion. He or she may also be given a service assignment at church—such as helping to usher, keeping flowers weeded, playing for the offertory, etc.

If your church doesn't participate in milestone celebrations, plan your own special event for your family. This could be something you and your children look forward to all year, and you could incorporate it into something like a camping trip or a visit to somewhere unique. You could also ask the church staff if your child could be assigned a serving responsibility at the church.

CHAPTER 5

MIDDLE SCHOOL
(AGES 11–14: SEVENTH AND EIGHTH GRADES)

MASTER LIFE THREAD: DESTINY (GENESIS 45:4–10)

Therefore, I urge you, brothers, in view of God's mercy, to offer your bodies as living sacrifices, holy and pleasing to God—this is your spiritual act of worship. Do not conform any longer to the pattern of this world, but be transformed by the renewing of your mind. Then you will be able to test and approve what God's will is—his good, pleasing and perfect will.

ROMANS 12:1–2

Think back to your middle school years.

Do you remember despairing because you wore a black shirt when everyone else wore blue?

Do you remember that microscopic zit that kept you from popularity, athletic prowess, fame, fortune, *and* being invited to Tiffany Engelson's birthday party?

Do you remember the devastation when you didn't make the basketball team, and the other guys—who you thought were your friends—laughed at you?

All right, maybe your horrifying moments don't match the ones above, but if you were a normal middle schooler, you had your own horrifying experiences.

Usually middle school doesn't generate life's best memories.

We often hear the term *staggering statistics*. These middle school statistics easily fit into that staggering category:

- A 76 percent increase in suicides by ten- to fourteen-year-olds has been reported by the Centers for Disease Control and Prevention.
- After dealing with the pregnancies of seventeen middle schoolers, a Maine school district voted to supply birth control to its students without requiring parental permission.
- At least 14 percent of adolescents are self-mutilators, and some researchers think that number could be as high as 39 percent, according to the *Journal of Abnormal Psychology.*
- Ten percent of students nationwide have tried marijuana before the age of thirteen, according to the Substance Abuse and Mental Health Service Administration.

Even for the most secure kids, the shower of pressures and hormones raining down on them can be difficult to navigate.

Typical responses by middle schoolers in our Biggest Question Survey reflected this middle school instability: "Why did God give me the parents He did?" "Why do I look this way?" "What's my purpose?"

As parents, we find the answer to the chaotic middle school years in the person of the Lord Jesus Christ—in His grace, His love, and His forgiveness. Our relationship and identity with Him are beyond value.

So far, the life threads we've focused on include respect for God's authority, gaining godly wisdom, and understanding God's grace and reflecting that grace in our relationships. As young teenagers identify with these godly characteristics, they should begin to understand the *destiny* God has planned for them *if* they seek His will. A life lived in obedience to the Lord is well beyond any temporal earthly destiny. This message is one of great hope, but we must teach it with great patience and sensitivity to their mixed-up, chaotic, will-I-ever-feel-good-about-myself delicate feelings.

Our goal with middle school children is in two parts:

1. That they recognize who they are in Christ

2. That they desire God's will for their lives

Philippians 2:12–16 speaks to both these points:

> Therefore, my dear friends, as you have always obeyed—not only in my presence, but now much more in my absence—continue to work out your salvation with fear and trembling, for it is God who works in you to will and to act according to his good purpose. Do everything without complaining or arguing, so that you may become blameless and pure, children of God without fault in a crooked and depraved generation, in which you shine like stars in the universe as you hold out the word of life—in order that I may boast on the day of Christ that I did not run or labor for nothing.

That passage leads to this outline:

1. Recognizing who we are in Christ:
   —A person whom God uses to do His will
   —A child of God
   —A person who shines like a star in the middle of a crooked and depraved generation

2. Desiring God's will for our lives:
   —In being obedient to Him
   —In being blameless and pure before Him
   —In holding forth the Word of Life

How's that for a challenge? We must steer our children through the barrage of peer pressure, media hype, mood changes, and lonely feelings so they become shining stars. What better destiny could there be than that?

Continually remind your teenager of his value:

- God gives him purpose.
- God gives him meaning.
- God gives him significance.

And continually pray for your teenager:

I keep asking that the God of our Lord Jesus Christ, the glorious Father, may give you the Spirit of wisdom and revelation, so that you may know him better. I pray also that the eyes of your heart may be enlightened in order that you may know the hope to which he has called you, the riches of his glorious inheritance in the saints, and his incomparably great power for us who believe. That power is like the working of his mighty strength. (Ephesians 1:17–19)

WHAT THEY'RE LIKE:
CHARACTERISTICS OF MIDDLE SCHOOLERS

Middle school can be a difficult time even for well-adjusted teenagers. So much is happening in their lives physically and emotionally. Everything goes crazy. Think back to your own middle school years, and you begin to understand what your children are facing (although our own painful memories may have blurred with time).

Think about the following characteristics of a middle schooler as you teach your own child.

1. *Middle schoolers are figuring out their place in life.* We know each of us is God's unique creation, and we hope our teenagers know that too. Yet how often do we tell them we consider it a privilege to be their parent? How often do we remind them how important they are to the Lord? How often do we encourage them to willingly submit to the plans the Lord has for their lives? Children in middle school are hungry for attention, reassurance, and love.

2. *Middle schoolers often express themselves by actions rather than words.*

Your seventh-grade daughter might not say she's sorry after an argument, but as an apology she starts setting the table, taking the time to fold the napkins into swans.

Your eighth-grade son walks across the kitchen and intentionally runs into you; he's not being clumsy; he's showing his love in the least embarrassing way (for him). Instead of yelling, smile and push him back (gently, of course).

As parents, we need to be sensitive to our young teenagers, understanding that they struggle to express themselves. Send them an e-mail or stick a note in their lunch, reminding them of your love and of God's love. Some days they might feel as if they're drowning in a vat of pudding, but in God's eyes they're always valuable. We need to encourage them to yield to His will and recognize that their destiny is serving Him.

3. *Middle schoolers struggle for independence, and sometimes that causes family conflict.* Your child wants to go somewhere you don't want her to go or wants to do something you don't want her doing. Most of the time we parents make good decisions, but sometimes we can be overprotective. We need to let our children express their independence in appropriate ways. Independence doesn't happen on their eighteenth birthday; independence is a process. We must allow them to make choices with our guidance until they can make wise choices without it. Someday (in a few short years), they'll be on their own. Our goal is to train them to be godly adults who know, love, and serve the Lord.

4. *Middle schoolers understand that wrong behavior has consequences.* Middle school teenagers understand that there are consequences to behavior. "If I study, I'll do well on the test." (That doesn't mean they will study, but at least they understand they should.) "If I sneak out of the house at night, I could be in danger."

On the other hand, they want instant gratification. Even though they know they'll feel sick if they drink another soda, they'll drink it because they want it (and will worry about feeling sick later). Or they know they need to complete the paper for school, but they'll spend their time downloading songs and worry about the paper in the morning.

Remind them that perseverance and patience are godly characteristics.

5. *Middle schoolers enjoy close friendships.* They say they want to be different, but then they'll dress the same way, act the same way, and use the same slang words as their friends. Peer pressure is a big deal, but it can be good as well as bad. God created friendship (Proverbs 13:20). Encourage friendships with teenagers in like-minded families. Challenge your child to be a leader instead of a follower. Encourage him to be one who pressures his peers in a good way.

6. *Middle schoolers worry about being normal.* As adults we laugh. Our teenagers think they look normal because they look like everyone else—even though now the whole group of them looks abnormal. Parents need to choose their battles. What's more important—that he's wearing his ugly neon-green shirt to Bible study or that he actually enjoys attending Bible study?

7. *Middle schoolers focus on themselves.* They can spend hours deciding what color fingernail polish to wear. They can make a colossal popcorn mess while they're watching TV and never notice that *someone* needs to clean it up. They can act like the world's coming to an end because Dad said no text messaging during dinner. Dinner is family time.

Direct your teenager's focus away from herself and toward others (starting with her own family members) by getting her involved in a church or community service project.

8. *Middle schoolers think others are judging them.* Because middle schoolers are self-centered, they live in constant fear that others are critically assessing them. How many parents have suffered through their teenager's mood changes "because so-and-so didn't say hi to me today."

I remember my daughter coming home from a middle school event concerned about something she'd said. She was sure everyone was now talking about her. I told her, "No, your friends aren't concerned about what you said, because they're thinking about the silly thing *they* said. They aren't thinking about you; they're thinking about themselves."

9. *Middle schoolers have a lot of questions about right and wrong.* If they attend public school (or sometimes even a Christian school), they're hearing things from their teachers that they aren't hearing at home. If they're on a sports team or they're friends with kids in the neighborhood, they're hearing words that aren't said at home. Parents need to have open, honest discussions with their teenagers, showing them answers from God's Word. Remind them of the sovereignty of God. He created a perfect world with perfect order, but people have messed it up; right is often seen as wrong and wrong as right.

Middle schoolers are on the brink of making a lot of big decisions in their lives, and they have a lot of questions. Are abortion, homosexuality, and premarital sex *really* wrong? If so, *why?* Parents need to guide with clear Bible-based answers that teach what God's will is in such situations. If we don't have honest talks with our kids, we won't have the opportunity to present God's answers, and we leave our children vulnerable to wrong choices.

10. *Middle schoolers want to do great things.* Young teenagers will tell you their grandiose plans for the future: They want to be presidents, musicians, astronauts, and basketball stars. Yet deep inside they wonder if they can do anything. We need to remind them of the spiritual gifts given by God.

WHAT THEY'RE ASKING:
QUESTIONS MIDDLE SCHOOLERS HAVE ABOUT GOD AND THE BIBLE

Many of the middle school questions were self-centered—something we didn't find in the younger grades. They wanted to know why they were here and wanted to understand their purpose in life. The apologetic questions (defense of our faith) that we saw with the third to sixth graders also continued.

This age is also fascinated with eschatology and when given the chance as to what to study in a class will often suggest the book of Revelation.

Here are middle schoolers' top questions and some help with the answers:

1. *What's the purpose of my life?*

As Christians, we're sanctified (set apart). We're set apart *from* something and set apart *to* something. We're set apart *from* those things that are wrong and set apart *to* serve God. He wants us to be useful to Him—whether we're tall, short, fat, skinny, shy, or funny looking or think we have a talent deficiency. As the verse says, "He will be an instrument for noble purposes, made holy, useful to the Master and prepared to do any good work" (2 Timothy 2:21).

2. *Why doesn't God answer my prayers?*

This is a big question for kids and one of the top questions for middle school students. So many kids (and adults) are confused about prayer. We all have questions about it, but we also know some answers straight from God's Word.

- God doesn't answer prayers that are opposed to His guidelines. Paul wrote to the Colossians that he prayed for them "that you may live a life worthy of the Lord and may please him in every way: bearing fruit in every good work, growing in the knowledge of God" (Colossians 1:10).

- God answers prayer according to His will. We read in Romans 8 that we don't know what we ought to pray, so the Spirit is our go-between, interceding for us in accordance with God's will (Romans 8:26–27). Other verses also emphasize that we're to pray according to God's will (1 John 5:14–15; Ephesians 5:17).

- We're to pray in the name of the Lord Jesus Christ. Praying in His name means more than just tacking "in Jesus' name" onto the end of our prayer. It means remembering that the only way to God is through His Son. If we say something in someone's name, we're submitting ourselves to that person's authority, so praying in Jesus' name means we're submitting to His authority. He represents us before God the Father. (Also see What Not to Do under Older Elementary.)

3. *Why do bad things happen to good people?*

When Adam and Eve sinned, the entire perfect world got messed up. Bad things happen because of sin. Sin affects people's behavior, nature, the weather, and the way things fall apart—it's all one big mess

(John 16:33). Christians have trouble just like everyone else does—but they shouldn't be discouraged. Even though bad things happen in all our lives, God promises to help us face those tough times (1 Peter 5:7). We shouldn't worry, but instead leave our troubles in God's hands (Philippians 4:6).

4. *What about the Holy Spirit?* What does He do?

- We're baptized by the Spirit (Colossians 2:12).
- We're filled by the Spirit (Galatians 5:16).
- The Holy Spirit is our intercessor (Romans 8:26).
- We're sealed by the Spirit (Ephesians 1:13).
- Other people should see the fruit of the Spirit in our lives (Galatians 5:22–23).

WHAT YOU CAN DO:
SUGGESTIONS FOR HELPING YOUR MIDDLE SCHOOLER GAIN A PERSONAL SENSE OF *DESTINY* IN GOD'S WILL

What about Salvation?

Young teenagers can easily understand the gospel message. If you've been consistently teaching your child the Bible since he was little, he most likely has trusted Christ by now. But there are exceptions, and maybe your teenager hasn't made the choice to accept God's gift of salvation. Encourage your teenager, but understand that the Holy Spirit is the One who ultimately convicts.

If your child out and out tells you he doesn't want to trust Christ, ask him why. Some teenagers simply refuse as a means of asserting control over their parents. Instead of understanding how their refusal affects their own life, they're focusing on what it's doing to you. Other teenagers may refuse because they don't want to think about it. The subject is too serious. And there are others who may have spent most of their growing-up years daydreaming or goofing off and truly haven't gotten the message.

Answer your middle schooler's questions with a gentle spirit. Let him know how excited you are about your own relationship with Christ. (Of course, if you aren't excited, that may be part of the problem.) Don't break down the lines of communication, but continue to be there for him.

Ideas and More Ideas …

1. *Attend meetings that introduce parents to your church's vision for supporting you as you spiritually nurture your teenagers.*

2. *Attend your church's meeting for parents where staff members and experienced parents give ideas for spiritually training teenagers.* Time may be set aside during this meeting for you to complete your family itinerary for the year. If not, fill it out at home as soon as possible. Your middle schooler is also old enough to take part in the planning—and to help teach her younger siblings. So involve your teenager, allowing her to make suggestions.

3. *Join a small group or Sunday school class where you can share with other middle school parents.* Get together throughout the year for family events. Make sure you include single parents. Study Titus 2, where Paul gives Titus a list of qualities the older men and women are to teach the younger men and women.

4. *Choose a family verse for the year.* Involve your middle schooler in this decision. In fact, you could challenge her to choose two or three verses, and the family votes on which one to use. Remind her that the verse needs to focus on doing God's will and, therefore, maturing toward the destiny God has designed for her.

5. *Continue or establish a relationship with a mentor/prayer partner.* This could be someone the church assigned your child back when he was in second grade. (See early elementary milestone celebration.) This person is primarily an encourager, and that role could look different, depending on your family's situation. Some in this position may offer only prayer support. Others may be more involved in the child's life, actually helping the child learn about the Bible or memorize verses.

6. *Ask your teenager what he learned at church.* Do this in a nonconfrontational way. You could talk about what you learned and then ask what he learned. Even if you listened to the same message, you may remember different points.

7. *Plan a different kind of family night than when your teenager was younger.* Work together on a big project. Your daughter might be interested in scrapbooking the family vacation. Your son might enjoy helping his dad work on the car. Or maybe your entire family would enjoy working together on building a doghouse or setting up an obstacle course. Or you may want to get out of the house and go minigolfing or hiking. Talk while you're working or playing together. Then come together for a special snack and a time of prayer and Bible study.

If your teenager is the oldest of several children, enlist his help in planning family nights for the younger children.

8. *Do a Bible study with your teenager on the will of God.* What is it? How do you find it? God tells us His will in the Bible. That doesn't mean that every last detail of our lives corresponds to a chapter and verse. But much of God's will can be answered by chapter and verse. Discuss situations and what the Bible says about them.

9. *Encourage your teenagers to think through what they believe.* Have family discussions around thought-provoking questions:

- Why are you glad you're a Christian?
- What difference does being a Christian make in your life?
- What do you think about the decision the school board made about the after-school prayer group? Do you think that's right or wrong? Why?
- I know that music group claims to be Christian. Do you think their lifestyle hurts them? Why or why not?
- Do you think a middle schooler can make a difference for Christ? How?
- Why do you think those kids at school got busted for doing drugs? Why would a kid take drugs, knowing how they mess up your body and mind?

10. *Talk about destiny.* What does it mean? How do you get to your destiny? *Destiny* is defined as your preordained future. Joseph (in Genesis 37—50) was destined to become great—and he did that by doing the best job at the moment:

As a boy, he obeyed his father.

As a slave, he obeyed Potiphar.

As a prisoner, he became friends with those around him.

And as a brother, he showed forgiveness.

Challenge your teenagers to do the best job possible wherever they are in life—whether it's at school, with their friends, on a sports team, or at church.

11. *Choose a book of the Bible to study in depth.* You can do the study together as a family, or parents and teenagers can study the book individually and then come together to discuss it. Don't hurry the study. Take all year if necessary.

Choose a name for your study that reflects the book's theme. (For instance, you might call a study on Ephesians "Wise Walkings.")

Determine the key word of the book.

Choose key verses from each chapter.

Choose one key verse for the entire book.

Do some research on the author God used to write the book (if known).

Look up words that aren't familiar.

Finally, talk and pray about how you could apply the book to everyday life.

12. *Understand that your young teenager is caught between childhood and adulthood.* Give her responsibilities, and if she carries through on those, give her more. As you talk to her about doing God's will, remind her that right now His will for her is to do whatever she does (and a lot of what she does includes school) with excellence and a good attitude.

As my husband often told the children and teenagers in our church, "You can look forward to the future and the job God will have for you as an adult—but right now, school is your job, and God's will for you is to do your best."

13. *Use car time wisely.* Middle school kids aren't driving, so they're still dependent on you to get them places. Turn off the cell phone and prohibit text messaging while you drive and chat. Discuss school, church, life in general, and the Lord. Just today I had a great car conversation with a teenager as we discussed a Bible character and the good choices that character made.

14. *Buy a Bible software program for your computer.* (I mentioned this earlier; it's important.) Yes, it will cost you a little bit, but it can be invaluable to you and your teenager. With a few clicks, you can see several Scripture versions, including Greek and Hebrew. You can check a concordance, a Bible dictionary, and a Bible encyclopedia. You can see maps and photos. Having the information right there on the computer will encourage your teenager to look up words he doesn't know or find answers to questions he might have.

15. *When you tell your teenager she can't do something, tell her why.* You need to respect her feelings and give an explanation. For instance, your daughter asks to go to Jana's fourteenth birthday party. Most of the eighth graders in town are invited to meet at the beach for a good time of fun that night. You have no desire for your daughter to be part of it. You've met Jana's mother; you know she thinks it's cool to allow kids to participate in inappropriate activities, such as watching R-rated movies or drinking beer. You also know she doesn't stay around to oversee her daughter's parties.

Explain it to your daughter: "Thirty teenagers and no adults on the beach after dark isn't something we feel comfortable allowing you to do. Last time the kids had a party at the beach, there was alcohol involved, and the boys vandalized some boats. This is just not a place where we want our daughter."

The discussion is over. Don't turn the decision into a debate.

16. *Go beyond the no.* When you prohibit your teenager from doing something her friends are doing, put another activity in its place. When we stop with the no, we put our teenager in the position of having to explain things to her friends *and* sitting home the night of the party, feeling lonely because everyone else is at the beach.

So go beyond the no by saying, "We don't want you attending the party, but I have an idea. I know you wanted to go into the city to see a musical. Let's do it that night." Or, "I don't want you attending Jana's party, but Uncle Steve and Aunt Kelli have been asking us to go up to their place some weekend to hike in the mountains. They said next weekend would work."

This philosophy won't solve all problems, but I know from personal experience (having been a parent of a couple of middle school students) that it works. You're helping your teenager to focus on a fun activity and giving her a graceful way to tell Jana she can't go to her party.

17. *Discuss God's will in regard to societal issues.* Your teenager probably has questions about many situations: homosexuality, abortion, premarital sex, drugs, alcohol, etc. Make it easy for your teenager to talk to you. Discuss the facts from a biblical point of view and in a calm manner. Check with your church to see what resources it has available to aid you in presenting the facts with clarity.

18. *Send your child a letter* (not an e-mail; he may want to save it) saying how much you enjoy him, that you consider it an honor and privilege to be his parent, and that you're praying he'll follow God's will in his life and make good choices now and in the future.

19. *Hike with your teenager, build or cook something together, enjoy a sport together, find a joint hobby.* As you spend time with your teenager, talk. Talk about the weather; talk about school; talk about the Lord; talk about life … talk, talk, talk. Enjoying an activity makes the atmosphere stress free and generates good feelings and communication. (In fact, a parent-teenager project could be one of the goals on your family itinerary. And, as we mentioned above, a project could be part of your family night.)

Often when I arrived home from junior high, Dad would stop working for a while and challenge me to a few games of Ping-Pong. (He was a pastor and so was often home studying in the afternoon.) I remember him talking to me about everything from choosing a mate, choosing a God-honoring career, being strong in my faith, to doing well in school. Those conversations while the ball bounced back and forth eliminated the teenage angst present in other conversations. I remember those times only as good—and I learned to play Ping-Pong fairly well.

Have you noticed that many of our parent suggestions focus on the need to communicate with your middle schooler? That's because the best way to guide your young teenager is one-on-one communication.

20. *Talk to your teenager at bedtime.* This is still a good time to talk with your child even though he's a teenager. Use those last few minutes after the computer or TV's off and he's ready to turn in for the night. Share some potato chips or a piece of cake. Or visit his room after the lights are out and sit on his bed and chat for a few minutes. Sometimes teenagers find it easier to share in the dark.

Pray with him. If he doesn't want to take a turn praying out loud, respect that. Don't use the prayer to review his faults or preach at him. Thank God for giving you the privilege of parenting such a great kid. Pray that he'll be a good example to others. Pray that he senses his destiny in doing God's will.

21. *Encourage your teenager to develop his own moral code of standards.* In the next couple of years, your child will face a lot of temptations. Study the subject of purity together and how keeping pure is God's will. Talk about what's right and what's wrong. Set some dating standards now (however your family plans to handle it).

Give your teenager a journal, and have him write down the standards he wants to set for his own life in light of God's will (with Scripture backup). Tell him you won't read it (unless he wants you to), because this is between him and the Lord. But he does need to show you that he's done what you've asked.

Why is this important? Because writing down his standards now is preparation for the future. When teenagers face a situation they've never thought about, they can have difficulty making the right choice on the spur of the moment. If teenagers think through what to say and do when tempted, they'll have their defenses in place. When they think about what's right beforehand and write it down, they'll be better prepared.

22. *Teach your teenager that he's not too young to pray about his choice of a future mate.* Suggest that he make a list of what he wants in a future spouse. (And promise him you won't look at it unless he wants you to.) Encourage him to choose someone who also has a sense of destiny in doing God's will in life.

A good, biblical first step is dating only Christians. Unfortunately, many young people mess up God's plan for their lives by choosing mates who discourage them or take them away from the destiny found in following the Lord.

23. *Encourage your teenager to get to know the pastor.* Invite the pastor's family to your house for dinner or take them out for dinner. The way a middle schooler relates to his pastor will make a big difference in his enthusiasm toward church. If your teenager has a question you can't answer, encourage him to talk to the pastor. Or tell him he can ask the question while the pastor's family is over for dinner. If your church is large, you may choose to invite the youth pastor or one of the associate pastors instead. But you need to connect your teenager to at least one church staff member or godly adult who attends your church. The way a teenager relates to godly adults during this time of life can make a big difference in his attitude toward church in the future.

24. *Do a family service project together.* Collect pennies for the local pregnancy center, serve meals to the homeless at a local mission, collect Bibles for an international mission agency, or rake leaves for the elderly.

25. *Get to know a missionary family.* The next time your church asks for homes for visiting missionaries, open yours. If possible, choose a family that has a young teenager. Encourage your teenager to keep in contact with the missionary teenager through e-mail even when the family goes back to the country where it serves.

26. *Ask your middle schooler: If you could serve the Lord in any way possible, what would you want to do?* Fly airplanes to distant, war-torn villages? Design a Web site of Christian resources? Write an animated children's series? Manage an overseas orphanage? Challenge your teenager to work toward her goal. Even at this age she can read about missionary pilots, learn how to design a Web site, purchase a DVD explaining animation, and work with children at church.

BIOS AND VERSES:
SUGGESTED BIBLE VERSES AND BIOGRAPHIES TO TEACH YOUR MIDDLE SCHOOLER

You may want to coordinate these discovery topics and memory verses with what the church is focusing on in its ministry to middle schoolers.

With your child now in middle school, your teaching approach should be different from what you were doing when he was eight or ten. (Nothing annoys a middle schooler more than being treated like a young child.)

Biographies

The situations in these biographies differ, but most of these people faced danger—as slaves in a foreign country, as a victim thrown into a lions' den, as a queen positioned to save an entire nation. In most cases, they did the best they could at whatever they were doing—whether it was working for a foreign official or serving time in prison. They had a sense of destiny and purpose in doing God's will.

1. *Joseph* in Genesis 37—50. Once again, review his biography—this time going through the account chronologically. Joseph's life began in a dysfunctional family. Yes, his family started out together, but his brothers obviously had a problem with him—so much so that they sold him into slavery. Joseph never forgot his family, nor did he forget God. His life reflected characteristics of obedience, patience, and forgiveness. He was destined to become great—and he did.

2. *Caleb* in Numbers 13. He was one of twelve spies sent out by Moses into the Promised Land. We suggested studying Caleb before—back in the early elementary ages—but he's worth looking at again. He's a good example of someone who did the best he could at what he was doing. Even though ten of the twelve spies said the people were too big and intimidating, Caleb understood that this was the land God had promised the Israelites. God, in His faithfulness, would take care of the giant people and all the other intimidating things that frightened the other spies. Caleb's destiny was the privilege of being allowed to enter Canaan. "Because my servant Caleb has a different spirit and follows me wholeheartedly, I will bring him into the land he went to, and his descendants will inherit it" (Numbers 14:24).

3. *Noah* in Numbers 27:1–11. No, not *that* Noah; this one's a *girl* named Noah who had four sisters: Mahlah, Hoglah, Milcah, and Tirzah. They lived back in the time of Moses, when sons were the ones who received the inheritance. So when Noah's father died, the girls were left with nothing. They had no brothers and no money. They could have sat around and felt sorry for themselves. But these girls were destined to go down in history for making a bold and brave request. They went to Moses and said that since there weren't any brothers and the family name was about to disappear, they needed a special inheritance. Moses listened to them and went to the Lord about the matter. The Lord told Moses to honor their request.

We don't know much about Noah and her sisters, but we do know they did what was right at the moment (and God saw it as important enough to record in His Word). Why choose this Noah to study? Middle schoolers enjoy learning little-known facts.

4. *David* in 1 Samuel 16 and continuing through the rest of 1 and 2 Samuel. David, too, was destined for greatness, but his father didn't think so. When God told Samuel to go to Jesse's home and

anoint one of his sons as future king, Jesse didn't even bring David to the get-together. Samuel had to remind Jesse about his other son. Yes, David was a sinner—like all of us—but he never forgot the mercy of God. Destined for great things? Not only did he become king, but Christ was born in the line of David. God chose to tell us of David's good choices, his bad choices, and his continual dependence on God.

5. *Esther* in the book of Esther. The biography of Queen Esther appeals to teenagers (especially girls) for a couple of reasons. Esther was beautiful, bold, and brave. A young girl wins the favor of a king and finds herself in the palace. "And who knows but that you have come to royal position for such a time as this?" (Esther 4:14). No, your daughter won't suddenly find herself queen of a country, but could she be in her school *for such a time as this?* Could your son be on that sports team *for such a time as this?* Could your family be on that missions trip *for such a time as this?*

6. *Daniel* in Daniel 1. Daniel was handsome, intelligent, hardworking, and faithful. Sometimes we forget that he (like Joseph) was taken from his country, friends, and family yet still did not forget the Lord. Nothing made him waver from his faith in God—even the threat of a night in the lions' den. Again, he did the best he could at whatever he was doing.

7. *Jonah* in the book of Jonah. Jonah had a destiny set before him—an actual destination. Here's the bio of a man who chose not to do God's will but rather to go his own way. After that, nothing about Jonah's life seemed easy. Floating around inside a fish certainly can't be fun, and sitting in the sun feeling sorry for yourself certainly doesn't sound appealing either. This is a man who paid a price for determining to be out of God's will instead of in it.

8. *Philip* in Acts 8. Philip was a leader in the Jerusalem church when trouble started. After Stephen was killed, Christians were systematically persecuted, causing many of them to flee the city. (In itself, this turned out to be a good thing, because more and more people heard the gospel as these men from Jerusalem began preaching in the outlying areas.) Philip began preaching in Samaria, and crowds of people came to hear him. But God had destined something different for Philip. He sent an angel to tell Philip to go down to the desert.

Philip might have wondered why God took him away from the crowds to travel a lonely desert road, but he obeyed. Once there, he met a man reading Isaiah. (How's that for an opening to witness?) Philip helped the man understand what he was reading, and the man trusted Christ. Turns out this man was basically the CFO of Queen Candace's Ethiopian Empire. God knew exactly where He wanted Philip to be, and Philip was willing to be there.

9. *Eunice* in Acts 16:1; 2 Timothy 1:5. God didn't speak to Eunice from a burning bush, nor was she thrown into a lions' den or swallowed by a fish. The only thing we know about her is that she was a great parent. (Maybe that's what your son or daughter is destined to be in life—an excellent parent.) She taught her son, Timothy, from the time he was little; and when he grew up, he became Paul's friend, helping him on his journeys and in the churches. Not only was Eunice destined to be a great mom, but she helped her son become whom God wanted him to be.

10. *Aquila* in Acts 18. Aquila was a tentmaker, an important job back in Bible times because some people actually lived in tents. Aquila and his wife, Priscilla, met the apostle Paul in Corinth (probably because Paul was also a tentmaker) and listened and learned as Paul talked about the Lord Jesus Christ. Paul moved to Ephesus, and Aquila and Priscilla went with him. Once there, they taught a VIP named Apollos and faithfully shared all Paul had taught them. Apollos then went on and taught others. Aquila's desire to serve God (even though he was a simple tentmaker) resulted in many people trusting Christ.

Memory Verses

Here are suggested verses to remind teenagers who God is and what His will is for their lives.

Deuteronomy 29:29. A reminder that God is God. We don't understand everything He says and does. He has secrets known only to Him. Instead of being concerned about what we don't know (and this can be a tendency of teenagers), we need to concentrate on what God *has* told us and pass along this good news to others.

Job 28:28. God's will for us is to praise and honor the Lord and stay away from evil.

John 5:24. God's will for us spiritually is to trust Christ as Savior so we receive forgiveness of sins and eternal life.

Romans 12:1–2. The teenage years are when many believers first dedicate their lives to the Lord. God's will for us is to present our bodies as living sacrifices evidenced by how we live.

First Corinthians 6:19–20. God's will for our bodies is to recognize that they're the temple of the Holy Spirit—He indwells us. We should respond by treating our bodies with care and by avoiding abusive habits (illegal drugs, premarital sex, etc.).

Philippians 4:8–9. God's will for our minds is to think about the good, positive things. Not everything that happens to us is good and positive, but God can use all things for His purpose. Our job is to depend on Him.

Ephesians 2:8–10. God's will for our lives is salvation through grace! That alone shows us how valuable we are to Him. Then He tells us we're His workmanship created in Christ Jesus for good works. Talk about a lofty purpose—that far exceeds earthly fame and fortune. Our purpose lasts for all eternity.

First Timothy 4:12. God's will for our daily walk is to be an example in what we say and do. Others are watching (a good thing to remember when we're faced with temptation).

First Timothy 6:17. God's will for our finances and possessions is to understand that money can be a good thing and can help us help others, but it shouldn't be the focus of our lives.

Philippians 3:14. This is God's will for our future. God has placed a goal in front of us. We need to keep our eye on the goal and move forward.

WHAT NOT TO DO:
COMMON ERRORS TO AVOID WITH MIDDLE SCHOOLERS

Middle school students can be self-centered, paranoid that others are judging them, and burdened with a confidence level hovering around zero. Of course, there are exceptions, but many middle schoolers feel this way.

Young teenagers need to see home as a safe place where they can freely be themselves without having parents always on their case. Home is where they're completely accepted even when they have a zit on their nose or they're wearing something that wasn't purchased at this week's "in" store.

Middle schoolers have a right to privacy. That means parents need to be extremely careful about sharing things that happen in their young teenager's life. We're encouraging you to participate in a small group with other middle school parents, but that doesn't mean that you break your child's confidences.

That's what sometimes happens.

"The girls are always texting my Johnny. He gets so embarrassed."

"Kara's struggling so much in math class. The teacher told us she just doesn't get it. I don't know where that kid comes from. None of our other kids had so much trouble in math."

"Alisa was so devastated when her face broke out last Saturday right before the Spring Fling at church. I had to push her out the door. She was in tears" (this in front of the parents of a model-perfect girl who totally intimidates your daughter).

This isn't sharing; this is gossiping—about our own children! Yes, all those verses about gracious speech and kindness include our relationships with our sons and daughters.

Do we realize that the other group members might tell their own kids about Johnny's girl problem or even make a comment themselves the next time they see Johnny?

Do we realize that our cruel words about daughter Kara can quickly get back to her?

Do we realize that those parents might tell their model-perfect daughter about Alisa's devastation over a zit? And wouldn't *that* make Alisa feel so much better?

Our teenagers need to know that what happens in the house stays in the house—and that includes warning siblings not to share personal information about each other. You're a family. You're a team. Family matters stay within the family.

Of course, there are times when you do speak about a child's problem with a pastor, teacher, or counselor. This is done in complete confidence, and it's a different situation altogether.

We don't have to guess what the Lord thinks about the matter. He tells us our words should be kind and seasoned with salt. He tells us we shouldn't gossip about others, and this applies to our kids as much as it applies to anyone else. His will is clear.

We talk about our children gaining our trust; we also need to gain and keep *their* trust.

CHECKLIST FOR PARENTS OF MIDDLE SCHOOLERS

How's your teenager doing? Here's a checkup to see how he or she is progressing.

As with the other checklists, not all these statements will fit all teenagers. This checklist is a guide for you, the parent, to evaluate whether you need to emphasize a particular area in your child's spiritual growth. Use the checklist to gauge what areas you may have missed so you can review those areas with your teenager. And use the blank lines to add your own areas to review.

Knowledge Commitments

___ My teenager knows that God is sovereign.

___ My teenager can list and explain several attributes of God.

___ My teenager understands the meaning of *destiny*.

___ My teenager knows that God reveals His will in His Word.

___ My teenager understands that the Old Testament focuses on humankind's need for a Savior and God's promise of the coming Messiah (the Lord Jesus Christ).

___ My teenager understands that the New Testament focuses on what happened when Christ came to earth, died, and was resurrected—and the church was established.

___ My teenager knows the earth came into being through creation, not evolution.

___ My teenager knows that once we're saved, we're always saved.

___ My teenager knows the biographies of most well-known Bible characters.

___ My teenager knows that his or her body is the temple of the Holy Spirit.

___ My teenager knows the importance of purity.

(Others:)

—

—

Love Indicators

__ My teenager shows love to God by desiring His will for his or her life.

__ My teenager shows love to God by respecting and obeying his or her parents.

__ My teenager shows love to God by studying His Word.

__ My teenager shows love by making good choices.

__ My teenager shows a desire to love God by committing His Word to memory.

__ My teenager shows love to God by choosing to stay pure.

__ My teenager shows love by praising God for who He is.

__ My teenager shows love to God by not abusing his or her body.

__ My teenager shows love to God by choosing good friends.

__ My teenager shows love to God by regularly talking to Him in prayer.

(Others:)

—

—

Service Activities

___ My teenager serves God by being a good example to others.

___ My teenager serves God by participating in church activities.

___ My teenager serves God by doing the best he or she can in all things.

___ My teenager serves God by having an attitude of thankfulness.

___ My teenager serves God by regularly reading and studying His Word.

___ My teenager serves God by showing kindness to younger brothers and sisters.

___ My teenager serves God by fulfilling responsibilities both at home and at church.

___ My teenager serves God by praising Him through music.

___ My teenager serves God by praying.

___ My teenager serves God by sharing his or her faith with others.

(Others:)

___

___

THE FAMILY ITINERARY FOR FAMILIES WITH A MIDDLE SCHOOLER

Make this plan fit *your* family. Now that your child is a facing his teenage years, he should be part of helping you design the itinerary.

While keeping a focus throughout the middle school years on a sense of destiny in desiring to fulfill God's will for your lives, each year you should study different verses or biographies.

As a parent, rededicate yourself to serving the Lord and desiring to do His will. Maybe you've been neglecting some areas in your own life, and you need to make the choice to get rid of some bad habits or change your attitude about some things. The family itinerary isn't just for kids!

Here are our spiritual goals for the year:

1.

2.

3.

4.

5.

6.

Our family verse for this year is:

We'll also study the following six additional verses (one every two months) about God and His character:

1.

2.

3.

4.

5.

6.

We'll also study the following three Bible biographies (one every two months):

1.

2.

3.

We'll study this book from the Bible:

Our title for this study:

The theme:

A new concept we studied:

A new word we learned:

A project we'll do together on family night is:

Our family will be involved in missions in these two ways:

1.

2.

Our family has completed this year's family itinerary and met our spiritual goals.

(Have each family member sign.)

PARTNERING WITH YOUR CHURCH

Be sure to look also at chapter 13 in part 2 of this book for ideas of how your church can partner with you in the middle school years of your teenager's life.

Notice especially the information there about a "milestone celebration." For middle schoolers, this needs to be different from the milestone celebrations for the younger children. This is a time of serious thought and dedication to the future—a time of encouraging your young teenager to dedicate himself or herself to serving the Lord, whether that's in full-time Christian ministry or as a person reflecting Christ in the secular workplace.

Even if your church doesn't give your child the opportunity to do this—you can talk to him about it. Encourage him to write down his thoughts in a journal or record them on video—something that will help him always remember the decision he made as a young teenager.

CHAPTER 6

HIGH SCHOOL
(AGES 14–18: NINTH THROUGH TWELFTH GRADES)

MASTER LIFE THREAD: PERSPECTIVE (GENESIS 50:15–21)

*But in your hearts set apart Christ as Lord. Always be prepared to give an answer
to everyone who asks you to give the reason for the hope that you have. But do this
with gentleness and respect, keeping a clear conscience, so that those who speak mali-
ciously against your good behavior in Christ may be ashamed of their slander.*

1 PETER 3:15–16

Your child is on the brink of adulthood, yet you occasionally still see glimpses of the little kid he once was. At other times, you gasp in amazement as he responds with astounding maturity.

Watching him or her, you sometimes wonder where your parenting skills went wrong, while at other times you're amazed at the young man or woman your child has become.

You want these last years together at home to be ones of seeing your teenager gain independence, confidence, and skills.

We want our teenagers to face the world knowing, loving, and serving God. We want them to be

Josephs, strong in their faith, no matter what's ahead on their life journey. We want them to understand that life is difficult, but also to rest in the life-supporting perspective that God is sovereign.

Perspective isn't an option. Everyone has a fully functioning perspective by which he lives his life. A teenager doesn't always think about perspective, but that's what guides how she survives at school, interacts with her friends, decides which boy she likes, or chooses what to put on her tray in the cafeteria line.

- A teenager whose perspective is "I must be the center of attention to be happy" will do anything to gain popularity, even if that means taking part in activities she knows are wrong.
- A teenager whose perspective is "I'll do anything to get into an Ivy League school" will pull all-nighters or perhaps cheat on a test to get the needed grades.
- A teenager with an "It's all worthless" perspective will give up or spend his time partying.

On this matter of perspective, Paul writes about three areas of concern.

> I want you to know how much I am struggling for you and for those at Laodicea, and for all who have not met me personally. My purpose is that they may be encouraged in heart and united in love, so that they may have the full riches of complete understanding, in order that they may know the mystery of God, namely, Christ, in whom are hidden all the treasures of wisdom and knowledge. I tell you this so that no one may deceive you by fine-sounding arguments. For though I am absent from you in body, I am present with you in spirit and delight to see how orderly you are and how firm your faith in Christ is. So then, just as you received Christ Jesus as Lord, continue to live in him, rooted and built up in him, strengthened in the faith as you were taught, and overflowing with thankfulness. See to it that no one takes you captive through hollow and deceptive philosophy, which depends on human tradition and the basic principles of this world rather than on Christ. (Colossians 2:1–8)

Look closer at these concerns:

1. *Understand that a biblical perspective is based on the sovereignty of God.* Colossians 2 is as true today as it was when Paul first wrote it. People were promoting deceptive and dangerous philosophies in attractive ways with wise-sounding words. (Think of new religions that have sprung up in recent

decades.) Our teenagers are bombarded by impressive ideas that sound right but are all wrong. Do we take the time to talk to our teenagers about what they're hearing at school, at church, in the media, on the Internet? Or are we too busy doing our own thing that we don't even pay attention?

2. *Understand that a biblical perspective matters in everyday life.* A biblical perspective applied to a teenager's daily life is not a list of rules handed down by Dad or Mom. The biblical perspective is a life lived with the assurance that our gracious, loving God is in control. He teaches us principles from His Word that give purpose, meaning, and significance.

By our example, we can convey to our teenagers that a biblical perspective is reasonable, logical, and founded on the revealed Word of God. The Bible has solid, satisfying answers to serious life questions. How do our teenagers see us living our lives? Do we have a biblical perspective when we're doing our taxes or are angry at the neighbors? Our teenagers are watching us.

3. *Understand that teaching a biblical perspective takes work.* Paul wrote that he struggled for the people. The word translated here as "struggle" comes from a Greek word meaning "agonize." Paul cared so much for the people he agonized over them. He wanted them to understand the goal of a biblical perspective. Could our teenagers say that about us? Do they see our earnest desire to see them submit to God's will? Or do they see us think about God only when we're sitting in a church pew?

We can't decide we're too busy to spend time with our kids.

We can't decide that it's not all that important.

We can't decide that making sure our teenager gets into the right college or finds the right job is a bigger priority than knowing and serving God.

The risks are too great. We have a job to do.

Nothing's more rewarding for parents than to see their children graduate from high school, attend college (or begin a career), choose a Christian mate, establish a home, and become active in a church … because we've helped them establish a biblical perspective.

WHAT THEY'RE LIKE:
CHARACTERISTICS OF HIGH SCHOOLERS

Many high school teenagers leave behind the insecurities of middle school and possess a growing confidence as they look toward the future. What will they do after high school? Who will they marry?

Where will they live? Should they be a lawyer or a landscaper? A missionary or machinist? (Maybe a missionary *and* a machinist?)

Lots of changes happen during these four years, and no two teenagers are exactly alike, but knowing some basic characteristics of these older teenagers can help us relate to them.

1. *They're at (or near) their peak physically, and this is often a point of pride.* Many are athletic. Use that to your advantage when planning service projects—in fact, you could promote *extreme* service projects where teenagers help with construction projects or run a kids' soccer camp. Put that physical energy to good use.

2. *They're on their way to becoming completely independent.* Yes, your son, who can dunk a basketball but can't hit the hamper with dirty laundry, will soon have to do his own laundry. Your daughter, who spends thirty minutes deciding whether to wear the blue or green shirt, will soon need to make decisions that can affect her entire life.

We can foster their independence by allowing our teenagers to make their own decisions when possible. (That doesn't mean you allow your fourteen-year-old to drive or your sixteen-year-old to stay out all night.) When he's faced with a big decision, sit down with him and talk about the pros and cons of all the options. Study the Bible, and see what God says about the subject.

3. *Teenagers are idealistic.* Your teenager may have grandiose ideas about changing the world. If he were president, he would declare no more taxes. If he were a teacher, he would spend one-on-one time with every student. If he were a doctor, he would find a cure for cancer. If he were a pastor, he would have a more-than-mega church.

Dreams are good, and a lot has been accomplished because someone had an idealistic dream. Use that idealism to plan a project. What would be the definitive family service project? What would be the greatest-ever teenager outreach project at church? Though he's suggested something that seems impossible … *is* it possible? Could you help him carry it through? What would it take? What would be the desired results?

At the same time, the world is not an idealistic place. He needs to have a sense of realism, to understand that life can be difficult and that not all our dreams come true. Yet God is sovereign. We need to keep His perspective when following our dreams.

4. *Teenagers can have a good sense of identity*—well, some of the time. Unlike their middle school brothers and sisters, many older teenagers are finding a sense of identity. Encourage that. Others still struggle and will continue to struggle during adulthood.

Our identity doesn't come from our name, our grades, our high school, our family, or our speed on the soccer field. Our identity comes from being a child of the sovereign God. He's our Creator. We can't begin to understand the depth of His love.

This is a reminder needed by the arrogant girl who thinks she's above all in beauty, popularity, and intelligence. Or by the shy boy who spends his time alone, wishing he had friends.

As Christians, we're brothers and sisters in Christ and part of God's family—and that's the very basis of our identity.

5. *Teenagers need to learn how to learn.* Sometimes high school and college are not so much about *what* we learn, but about learning *how* to learn. Kids discover how to research and study and come to a conclusion. Include Bible study in their quest for learning. Supply them with Bible software for their computers or a variety of study books, and show them how to research a Bible verse, character, or concept.

6. *Teenagers have increased concern for others.* Most high school students are somewhat self-centered, but many also are outwardly focused. They care about the orphans in Africa, the homeless people they see wandering the streets downtown, and the boy at school who has physical difficulties. Here's a great opportunity for a service project. Save money for the orphans, supply the homeless with food, encourage friendship with the boy at school.

7. *Teenagers place importance on friendships.* Parents can encourage good friendships by allowing their teenagers to take part in church activities and allowing their teenagers' friends to congregate in their home (with supervision, of course). Even some Internet social networks are okay. Ask your teenager for his password, and let him know you'll occasionally check out the site. Tell him that even though you trust him, you don't trust everyone else and that you simply want to know what's happening. Don't be overbearing about this, reading every word every friend writes, but do a quick overview. Or as one mom told me, "My youth pastor and his wife are both on it, and I know they're monitoring what the kids are saying. That gives me a feeling of security." That's good, but you can't leave it up to the youth pastor and his wife; you, too, need to know what's going on in your teenager's life.

8. *Teenagers need to be trusted.* And that can be difficult. It means they need their privacy, and parents shouldn't be snooping around their kids' rooms when they're at school. (An exception would be if the teenager has truly shown signs of taking part in an unsafe, immoral, or illegal activity.) Assume that your teenagers are trustworthy. If they break that trust, that's a different story. They must regain it. Otherwise respect their privacy.

When I was a teenager and on my way out the door, my parents would say, "Have a good time. We trust you." This did more to encourage me to make good choices than any lecture would've done. I wanted to maintain that trust.

9. *Teenagers need to be taught that sex is a gift from God reserved for marriage.* Teenagers get bombarded with sexual messages at school, in magazines, from TV programs, on the Internet—everywhere. Most of these messages are corrupted, telling the teenagers anything but "wait for marriage."

Be open and honest with your teenagers. Remind them that their body is the temple of the Holy Spirit, and that saving themselves for marriage is a precious gift.

10. *Teenagers should be challenged.* They've come a long way from that little baby you brought home from the hospital, and soon they'll be gone. We want our teenagers to go into the world with a biblical perspective based on the sovereignty of God. Don't leave that to chance, assuming they get the point. Talk about looking at the world around them with a biblical worldview. That includes the way we perceive friendships, look at art, think about science, watch movies or TV, handle difficulties, think about a career, and everything else in life. Take him to a worldview conference, or do a Bible study together—a good choice is the *God-Colored Glasses* elective published by 24-7 Ministries (Awana). Pray for your teenager—that he'll face the world as a young person who knows, loves, and serves the Lord.

WHAT THEY'RE ASKING:
QUESTIONS HIGH SCHOOLERS HAVE ABOUT GOD AND THE BIBLE

Once again, we see a shift in the focus of the questions. High school students want to know how to tell their friends about God. This is encouraging, as we see teenagers desiring to share their faith with others.

1. *My friends tell me that the Bible contradicts itself. What can I tell them?*

When someone says that the Bible contradicts itself, the best thing you can do is ask for an example.

- Most people (especially teenagers who would be challenging your teenagers) won't have an example. They're just telling you what they heard someone else say.

- Some people may bring up an event in the Gospels. In these situations, explain that the authors were eyewitnesses and related things from their individual perspectives. (If you and your friend both saw a car accident and the police asked for testimony, the two of you wouldn't say *exactly* the same thing. You would tell what you saw from where you were standing; your friend would give testimony from her perspective.)

- Some will compare an Old Testament regulation with the freedom we have in Christ as found in the New Testament. Explain that once the Lord Jesus Christ came to earth, died, and rose again, we no longer have need of the Old Testament sacrificial system. Christ is our sacrifice.

2. How do I explain that heaven and hell are real places?

If people don't believe that the Bible is the literal Word of God, they're likely to have trouble believing that heaven and hell are real places. Start with a confident statement that you believe the Bible and that since the Bible talks about heaven and hell being real places, you believe that they are.

Here are some facts that the Bible tells us:

- Hell is a place of eternal punishment (Revelation 20:15).
- Heaven is a place of eternal reward (Philippians 3:20).
- Heaven is a perfect home (Revelation 7:16–17).
- We'll have glorified bodies in heaven (1 Corinthians 15:51–52).

3. How can I know God's will for my life?

Sometimes we get the idea that God hides His will. But God is a lot more interested in our doing His will than we are.

That's why we have the Bible. The Bible tells us exactly how to live our lives. We're to be honest, obedient to God (and to those in authority over us), and kind. We're to have a good attitude and be content and thankful. Does the choice we're making align with those qualities?

We also know that God has given us spiritual gifts. Does the choice we're making use our gift?

If the answers to those questions is yes, then we're in God's will. But if our choice requires us to be dishonest or disobedient, then we're not in God's will.

Sometimes the choice is between two things that both seem right. Is everything working out for one possibility, but not for the other? Then do the one that's available. If both are strong possibilities and both seem right, then make a choice, and glorify God in whatever you choose. God wants us to live a godly life no matter what circumstances we choose.

WHAT YOU CAN DO:

SUGGESTIONS FOR HELPING YOUR HIGH SCHOOLER GAIN THE *PERSPECTIVE* THAT GOD IS IN CONTROL

What about Salvation?

High schoolers who have grown up in a Bible-believing, evangelistic church and have parents who consistently teach God's Word will know the importance of trusting Christ. Yet some still haven't taken that step.

Appeal to your high school student by challenging him to think. Be available for nonpreachy discussions. To be prepared for talking with your teenager, read books on biblical worldview that give statistics on manuscript and historical evidence for the Bible. Research information on creation and evolution and point out the inconsistencies in evolution. Study data on archaeological findings and how they consistently support the Bible's historical record.

Teenagers who trust Christ while in high school usually are thinkers. They understand there's something missing from their lives. Or all those things their parents or pastor has been telling them since preschool suddenly make sense.

Make sure your teenager consistently attends church. She might not want to, but you're still the parent. We don't allow them to neglect going to the dentist or doctor for their physical health, so why are some parents so willing to give up on their child's spiritual health? (Some parents make the difficult choice of changing churches during their child's high school years so their son or daughter is in a good youth ministry. Sometimes this choice is based on external factors, but I've known just as many parents who made the choice to get their child into a solid, Bible-based youth group, even when that group was a lot smaller than the previous church's group.)

Be honest. "Dylan, I hurt knowing that you haven't trusted Christ. I want you to know that I want our family to one day be together in heaven. My relationship with Christ means more to me than anything, and I want you to know Him too." (Of course, you need to live your life reflecting that joy because your teenager will be watching.)

Be gentle. You don't want to break the lines of communication. You want your teenager to continue talking to you.

Ideas and More Ideas …

1. *Develop your family itinerary with your high school student's help.* If possible, allow him to attend the parent-commitment night at church. Ask him what he wants to study. Ask your teenager what his biggest question is about God and the Bible. What part of the Bible does he wish he knew more about? Has he had someone ask him a Bible question he couldn't answer? This might be a question that came up during a witnessing situation with a friend or from a younger child your teenager was babysitting or even a younger brother or sister.

2. *Team up with other families that have high school students.* This not only encourages accountability but teenagers who have friends with similar house rules often lean on each other when obeying parental decisions. (For instance, when you tell your daughter she can't go to the concert, it helps when the Smiths and the Bensons tell their teenagers the same things.)

When our kids were in high school, we (along with two other families) took our kids out of school and went to Chicago for the day. We went to a conference at Moody Bible Institute, took a long walk around the city, and had a lot of fun. Our purpose was to have a good time together, but something else resulted from that trip: The daughters in all three families decided to attend Moody.

3. *Choose a family verse for the year*—or how about an entire chapter? Allow your teenager to choose a chapter he would like to memorize that focuses on the right perspective.

4. *If your teenager has had a relationship with a mentor/prayer partner, continue to encourage that relationship.* This friendship could continue after the high school years and be good support as your young adult makes life choices.

5. *Do a study on biblical worldview/perspective with your teenager.* Our worldview colors the way we watch television, read books, look at art, view history, interact with our friends, enjoy a bike ride—everything we say and do.

Discuss people in the news. What's their perspective or worldview?

6. *Join with other parents of teenagers to send your teenagers (or go with them) to biblical worldview weekends, creation/evolution seminars, and Bible studies on the importance of purity.* One church has a monthly worldview night. Though this is primarily for teenagers, parents are invited too. The purpose

of the evening is to encourage kids to have a right perspective on life. Resources from several different places are viewed, shared, and discussed.

7. *Encourage family members to have mutual respect for each other.* A biblical perspective includes treating family members correctly. Don't allow name-calling between siblings. Create a feeling of trust between you and your teenagers. "Yes, we expect you to tell us where you're going when you go out, but we'll also tell you where *we're* going." Knock on closed doors instead of barging in. Don't read personal journals that are left on the bed when your teenager leaves for school.

8. *Teach your teenager about prophetic events.* Many of the questions on the Biggest Question Survey centered around the future. From personal experience, I've seen eschatological questions come up over and over in discussions with teenagers. Sometimes, parents and teachers (and sadly, even pastors) skip the subject because they don't feel qualified to deal with it. But by skipping the subject, we're not giving our teenager the biblical base that he needs *and* desires. Ask your pastor for recommendations of good books. All kinds of stuff has been written on the subject, so you want to make sure you're starting from the right base—a good choice would be the *Revelation* elective published by 24-7 Ministries (Awana).

9. *Talk to your teenager.* I remember reading an article that focused on teenagers needing after-school talking time with parents even more than younger children do. Teenagers typically want to talk *immediately,* and if they have to wait a couple of hours, they retreat (for the most part) into themselves and won't do much talking. Even if your physical presence isn't possible, you can give a call on your cell phone.

10. *Spend one-on-one time with your teenager.* Moms should do this with sons and dads with daughters. Boys need to get a woman's viewpoint on issues; girls need to get a man's viewpoint. At another time, do just the opposite. Talk about the biblical perspective on current teenager issues.

11. *Liken sexual purity to a gift presented to your spouse—that's the way God designed it.* Teenagers are bombarded with the opposite message. Would you want a gift that was opened? Would you want a gift that was already given to someone else or even several other people? What's the meaning of a gift?

12. *Plan a reading schedule so the family can read the Bible through in a year.* You don't need to do this together—but you should all be on the same schedule. This not only ensures that everyone will stay on pace, but also gives you the opportunity to come together and discuss what you've read. Or you could purchase Bible CDs and listen to them in the car or while getting ready in the morning.

13. *Study Hebrews 11.* This Bible chapter lists people who had the right perspective. Discuss, as a family, the people who are listed there. Why were they included? Why is faith so important? Who do you know who lives now that you think could be included on the list?

14. *Ask your teenager to write down what he would like to be doing ten years from now.* Discuss how he can begin working toward those goals now. Put the list in a sealed envelope, and store it in a place where he can find it in ten years to see how many of the goals he reached.

I did this with a high school Sunday school class and kept the lists. Although many of the girls went off in various directions away from their original goals, one girl stayed right on track. What a fun surprise it was for her when my husband read it as he performed her wedding ceremony! He started the message part by reading the life goals Beth had written as a high school freshman. The great thing about Beth's list is that she had met her goals.

15. *If your child is college bound, discuss the possibility that he might not agree with everything that's taught.* (This can be true even in Christian colleges.) Talk about ways he can handle it, such as asking the professor questions and presenting his own view gently and nonconfrontationally. If he's attending a secular university, go with him to check out nearby churches that have college ministries. Also get a list of or connect with on-campus Christian ministries.

16. *Challenge your teenager to design a computer-programmed Bible quiz.* This can be something simple such as multiple choice or true and false, or if you have a technological whiz on your hands, he could include animation and action.

17. *Ask your teenager to make a Bible instruction book.* Challenge her to find twenty-five instructions God gives us in His Word. Encourage her to enter them in the computer (perhaps adding graphics), then print them, and keep them in her Bible.

18. *Make your home the center of activity.* Welcome your teenager's friends, so they feel comfortable. Stock up on inexpensive snacks (popcorn is good). Talk to them. Be interested (but not annoyingly so) in their lives. Share your faith with them or be willing to discuss issues. More than one adult credits the parents of a Christian friend for leading them to Christ or helping them navigate a tough situation.

19. *Pray with your teenager about his future.* Ask for wisdom for him to make good choices and stay strong in his faith. In your prayers for your teenager, adapt Paul's wording: "We have not stopped praying for you and asking God to fill you with the knowledge of his will through all spiritual wisdom and understanding" (Colossians 1:9).

20. *Volunteer to help the youth pastor.* Usually youth pastors (or volunteer leaders) are looking for adults to help during special activities. Volunteer. Not only does this give you an opportunity to see what's happening in your teenager's life, but this will give you an opportunity to get to know your child's friends. Your teenager will also see that you care about him enough to spend your Friday night

crammed on a hay wagon with forty-nine loud-talking, pushing-and-shoving, hay-throwing kids instead of sitting at home in comfort watching the football game.

21. *Choose one verse to write about.* Give everyone in the family a week to write a no-longer-than-five-minutes devotional about the verse, but no one's allowed to tell anyone else the approach they're taking. (Even younger kids can do this.) Come together on family night, and allow each person to give their devotional. You'll probably have as many different perspectives on the verse as there are members in your family.

22. *Be thankful for what others have done.* Part of a biblical perspective is thankfulness. As a family think of all the different people you know who consistently do their jobs and are never thanked. Think about the woman at the tollbooth who always gives you a friendly smile, the mail carrier, the woman who washes the linens in the church nursery, your neighbors, etc. Write thank-you notes as a family to at least ten people you've never taken the time to thank before.

23. *Ask the pastor if he would be willing for a couple of teenagers to hang out with him for a day.* They can visit with him, do office work, maybe even help out with a message. Have the teenagers take the pastor out for lunch. Teenagers can learn about the church from the pastor's perspective. Most pastors would enjoy this opportunity too.

24. *Plan a vacation with your family.* It doesn't have to be far away. Visit museums and national parks. Talk about the biblical perspective. Is the brochure that tells you how the canyons of the park came into being five million years ago written from a biblical perspective? Is the picture at the art museum that depicts Moses coming down from Mount Sinai representing a biblical perspective? Is the exhibit of strange-looking idols at the amusement park designed with a biblical perspective?

25. *Have your teenager look at the list of Bible biographies for the younger children.* Ask him to research one or two of the Bible characters and present the devotional for the family for the next couple of weeks.

BIOS AND VERSES:
SUGGESTED BIBLE VERSES AND BIOGRAPHIES TO TEACH YOUR HIGH SCHOOLER

As you plan your family itinerary, ask your high school student to choose the Bible characters to study. Teenagers need to do more than read a couple of verses and answer a few questions. Challenge your teenager to research historical and cultural information about the time and place where the Bible character lived. Look for people who had a perspective based on the sovereignty of God—a biblical worldview. Or choose people who had the opposite—a worldview based on their own selfish desires.

And if you can afford it, visit Israel with your teenager. Yes, it's expensive, but seeing the actual places where Bible events took place will make what they read in the Bible very real to them.

Biographies

1. *Joseph* in Genesis 37—50. By now your teenager should be familiar with the biography of Joseph. Review together why the qualities Joseph reflected in his life are good qualities to emulate in your teenager's life.

Joseph was a young and good-looking man, in control of a grand house. With his position came power and probably wealth. How easy it would have been for him to give in to Potiphar's wife—but he refused. He stayed away from her as much as possible, and when the temptation became too intense, he fled. That temptation was just as great for Joseph as the temptation is for your teenager to yield to pressure to do wrong. Yet, Joseph understood God was with him. He understood what choices he had to make. Pray that your teenager, too, will have the same determination to flee youthful lusts.

2. *Samson* in Judges 13—16. Here's an example of a young man who didn't have a biblical perspective. The Lord blessed him as he grew to manhood, but he insisted on doing things his own way. He grew proud and arrogant, and he was so caught up in the lust of the flesh that he was blinded to Delilah's trickery. Samson acted foolishly, and instead of learning his lesson, he went on to act even more foolishly. Talk about thickheadedness! Still God used him. Consider what this man's life might have been if he had consistently followed God.

3. *Job* in the book of Job. God gave Satan permission to torment this man, and Job lost all he had— land, money, servants, and all his family except his wife. Even then, Satan wasn't done—Job ended up with a nasty case of boils. His friends came to comfort him, but their idea of comfort was telling Job all he'd done wrong. Yet Job was confident that God was sovereign and refused to blame Him for his troubles. God rewarded Job for his faith, and Job gained more than he had before Satan's torment.

4. *Nehemiah* in the book of Nehemiah. He was a Jew serving in Persia as the king's cupbearer. When he heard about the devastation of the Jerusalem city walls, he obtained permission from the king to go to Jerusalem and rebuild the walls. The task wasn't easy, but he aimed for the goal and was able to

complete the task in fifty-two days—a testament to his leadership. Nehemiah had perspective. He knew what needed to be done, and he did what he could to do it.

5. *Obadiah* in 1 Kings 18:3–16. Obadiah was in charge of Ahab's palace—a godly servant in the midst of paganism. "Obadiah was a devout believer in the LORD" (1 Kings 18:3). When the wicked Queen Jezebel ordered the prophets of God to be killed, Obadiah hid a hundred of the prophets in a cave and made sure they had food. Obadiah grew up knowing God, as he himself testified: "I your servant have worshipped the LORD since my youth" (1 Kings 18:12). Obadiah understood the sovereignty of God and didn't waver in his worship, though he lived at a time when most (including the queen) worshipped Baal.

6. *Mary* in Matthew 1; Luke 1—2. Mary had the right perspective. Yes, she was afraid when the angel first approached her, but she quickly understood the task before her. She would be the mother of the Son of God. Wouldn't you like to meet Mary? Wouldn't you like insight into the character of this chosen woman?

7. *John the Baptist* in Matthew 3:1–9. John, a cousin of the Lord Jesus Christ, also had the right perspective. He lived a life dedicated to announcing the coming of the Lamb of God, the One who would provide a solution for the problem of sin.

8. *Matthew* in Matthew 9. He was a tax collector, a job synonymous with *cheat, liar,* and *thief.* But when he met Christ, instantly he made the choice to follow Him. As a first step in his discipleship program, he invited over his tax collector friends (plus some other scoundrels) for dinner so they, too, could see and know and hear the Son of God.

9. *Lydia* in Acts 16. She was a businesswoman with a lucrative trade—she sold purple cloth. She had money; she had a house; she had friends. She met with those friends by the river to pray, and when Paul joined them, she listened to his message and trusted Christ. She opened her house to him as a ministry base while he was in Philippi.

10. *Paul* in Acts and his letters. Paul's main focus was the persecution of Christians—until he had the eye-opening experience on the road to Damascus. Then his focus changed to that of preaching Christ. Follow Paul's missionary journeys, and learn about the people whom he led to Christ.

Memory Verses

Joshua 24:15. In not too many years, your high schooler may be married and starting a family. Hopefully, he'll desire to bring up his own children in the nurture and admonition of the Lord.

Psalm 100. Our perspective should be one of thanksgiving and praise for God's love and faithfulness. God is sovereign. This is what we've been teaching our children since they were preschoolers.

Psalm 119:9–12. Our perspective should be one of thirst for spiritual truth. Not only is Psalm 119 the longest chapter in the Bible, but its theme *is* the Bible. How does a young person do the right thing? By living according to God's Word. You could challenge your teenager to do further study in this chapter and write in her own words the psalmist's description of the importance of God's Word.

Micah 6:6–8. Our perspective should be one of daily walking with the Lord.

John 1:1–3. Our perspective should be one of recognizing that Christ is the Son of God. The Lord Jesus Christ (the Word) is with God and is God. He created the world; He was there from the beginning.

Romans 3:19–26. Our perspective should be one of understanding God's grace provided by Christ's death on the cross. This is a longer passage, but one that's valuable for understanding law and grace. These verses explain the difference between the Old and New Testaments.

Romans 12:9–17. Our perspective should be one of obedience to the Lord. Here's a list of rules for living. Since He's our Creator and He's in control—why would we *not* listen to Him?

Romans 15:4. Another reminder that the Scriptures were written to teach us what we need to know.

Galatians 5:22–23. Our perspective should be one of desiring to reflect the nine facets of the fruit of the Spirit in our lives.

Revelation 21:3–5. Our perspective should be one of hope in the future—all of eternity with our Savior in heaven.

WHAT NOT TO DO:
COMMON ERRORS TO AVOID WITH HIGH SCHOOLERS

High school students are getting ready to go out into the world. They're exposed to more and more things that you wish they never had to know or experience. Sometimes teenagers make bad (sinful) choices because of insecurity, immaturity, or out-and-out rebellion. (We're not excusing these choices—they're clearly sin and not God's will for your son or daughter.)

Bad choices need to be dealt with accordingly. But in dealing with the sin, many parents isolate themselves from the sinner. Instead of giving wise guidance on what to do to resolve the situation, parents angrily yell things that they can never take back—words such as "I wish you never were born. Why can't you be a good kid like your sister? You've been nothing but trouble since day one." A lot of times the angry words are a result of embarrassment on the parents' part: What will they tell their friends? How can they face the people at church? Didn't everyone consider them the perfect family?

Your child is still your child. He still needs your love despite his faults. Don't complicate one sin by heaping another (anger) on top of it. Think of David and all the trouble he got into—yet God loved him and used him to do great things.

Do what you can to keep the lines of communication open. The Lord tells us to bear the burdens of one another, to love one another, and to accept those who are weak (1 John 4:11; Romans 14:1; Galatians 6:2). Unfortunately, parents often apply such admonition to everyone but their own children.

So pray for them, talk to them, love them. Many adults are living for the Lord today because their parents showed them unconditional love during the tough teenage years.

CHECKLIST FOR PARENTS OF HIGH SCHOOLERS

Here's a checklist to see how you're doing. You can add to the list to tailor it to your family.

Knowledge Commitments

___ My teenager knows the importance of having a biblical perspective in all areas of life.

___ My teenager can summarize the biographies of the major Bible characters and tell whether they lived according to a biblical perspective.

___ My teenager knows about future events (eschatology).

___ My teenager knows that God shows love, anger, sadness, and joy and understands those same emotions in his or her own life.

___ My teenager knows there is external evidence for the Bible's accuracy and trustworthiness and can relate facts about that evidence.

___ My teenager believes that God created the heavens and earth and that evolution is flawed and can explain his or her reasoning.

___ My teenager understands that once we trust Christ as Savior, nothing can break that relationship.

___ My teenager knows that heaven and hell are real places.

___ My teenager understands the importance of sexual purity.

___ My teenager understands the difference between law and grace.

(Others:)

___

___

Love Indicators

__ My teenager shows love for God by having a biblical perspective and understanding that God is sovereign.

__ My teenager shows love for God by desiring to tell his or her friends about Christ.

__ My teenager shows love for God by seeking God's will for his or her life.

__ My teenager shows love for God by worshipping God through words and music.

__ My teenager shows love for God by regularly talking to Him in prayer.

__ My teenager shows love for God by reading the Bible and hearing what He says to us through His Word.

__ My teenager shows love for God by respecting and obeying his or her parents.

__ My teenager shows love for God by trusting Him even when things are tough.

__ My teenager shows love for God by making wise decisions even when that means standing alone.

__ My teenager shows love for God through obedience to Him.

(Others:)

__

__

Service Activities

__ My teenager serves God by being a good example.

__ My teenager serves God by sharing his or her faith with others and understanding that even when this is difficult, the Holy Spirit is within us and will give us courage.

— My teenager serves God by being a good example to younger brothers and sisters.

— My teenager serves God by cheerfully doing his or her part as a member of our family.

— My teenager serves God by regularly helping out at church.

— My teenager serves God by intelligently defending God's Word.

— My teenager serves God by being part of an outreach program.

— My teenager serves God by treating others with kindness.

— My teenager serves God by committing himself or herself to a life of service, whether in the Christian or secular workplace.

— My teenager serves God by teaching others about His Word.

(Others:)

—

—

THE FAMILY ITINERARY FOR FAMILIES WITH A HIGH SCHOOLER

This plan is different from those for earlier ages. You may find that what works best is doing Bible study individually and then coming together to discuss what you've learned. Be flexible. Develop a plan that accommodates the myriad of schedules. Or you could have your older teenager occasionally lead your family devotional time. Do what works well for your family.

Our spiritual goals for the year are:

1.

2.

3.

4.

5.

6.

Our family verse for this year is:

This year we'll do a family research project on the following:

(For this research project, choose one of the following, or choose a similar topic.)

- Apologetics—learning the facts that defend our faith.

- Creation/evolution—why we believe creation; the flaws in evolution.

- Archaeology—what are the most recent archaeological discoveries?

- Church history—a study of Bible manuscripts or of people who gave their lives for Christ.

- Political/cultural response to Christianity—what are the indications that Christianity isn't accepted by our society? What can we do about it?

We'll memorize this chapter from the Bible:

We'll read (either as a family or individually) the following books:

1.

2.

Our family service project this year will be:

Our family has completed this year's family itinerary and met our spiritual goals.

(Have each family member sign.)

PARTNERING WITH YOUR CHURCH

Be sure to look also at chapter 14 in part 2 of this book for ideas of how your church can partner with you in the high school years of your teenager's life and beyond.

Notice especially the information there about a "milestone celebration," which for high schoolers should be during a regular church service. This is a culmination of a lot of hard work, but it isn't the conclusion of these teenagers' spiritual growth; that's a process that continues throughout life.

If your church is involved in a program that supports families in the spiritual nurturing of their children, your teenager may be presented with a study Bible or Bible software program, along with a special inscription from the pastor or a staff member. During the celebration, the congregation will hear a short biography of your child and be given opportunity to pray for the future of your son or daughter.

AND BEYOND ...

The diploma is in your child's hand, and he's off to face the world.

Your job's done, right?

Wrong. The job continues for both you and the church.

My dad often was asked to speak on college campuses, with the assignment of defending Christianity—this was decades ago when the philosophy of free love, no guilt, and no God was prevalent among many college students. He challenged them to "give God equal time"—the premise being that if we think about and study the claims of the Bible as much as we research evolution or humanism or any other man-made philosophy, God's perspective will come out ahead.

But once they're on their own, many young people choose to reject everything their parents taught them. They ignore God completely and embrace a false belief system.

Giving God equal time is a principle as important today as it was four decades ago.

And so our job continues.

As a parent, you can do the following:

- Send messages of encouragement, whether your son or daughter is in college, starting a job, or in the military. The messages can focus on a verse, a concept, or a life-changing experience you had when you were young.

- Let him know of your continued prayers for him.
- Keep the lines of communication open even when she makes choices that cause you to cringe in despair.
- Be encouraging and interested in his life. Is he involved in a church? Does he work in a youth basketball program in the inner city or travel with a college singing group?
- Schedule time to visit the youth programs or attend concerts. Yes, that might mean a trip across the country, but you're showing him you care and that you're proud (in a good sense) of what he's doing.
- Welcome her new friends into your home. I remember our daughter bringing five college friends home with her the weekend of her twentieth birthday. Over dessert, one of the guys asked my pastor husband a question about something they were studying in Acts class. That question turned into a fun, three-hour discussion about the ministries of Peter and Paul.

Being a parent is hard work. Children don't grow into adults without guidance, and giving that guidance is an all-day, everyday job.

We want our children to grow into adults who become modern-day Josephs, reflecting the same qualities Joseph did:

- Respect for the awesomeness and authority of God.
- God-given wisdom based on their knowledge of God and His Word.
- Grace in their relationships with others.
- A great sense of destiny and purpose in doing God's will.
- An overall perspective on life that starts with the sovereignty of God.

We'll always be the parents of our children. Yet, there does come a day when we no longer have a say (though we may still have influence) over the choices our children make. We pray that we'll be able to look at our sons and daughters with pride (the right kind), because we see them knowing, loving, and serving the Lord. We've intentionally taught them the importance of doing God's will according to God's Word.

But our job still isn't done … because here come the grandchildren!

PART TWO
(ESPECIALLY FOR CHURCHES)

CHAPTER 7

WHY WE NEED EACH OTHER

Parents can do a great job of being the primary spiritual nurturers of their children, but they can be so much more effective if you, the church, are supporting them in the endeavor.

Remember too that a church can have great programs, great staff, and great Bible-based curriculum, yet the children may not apply the church-learned truths to daily life without the all-important spiritual teaching and encouragement in the home. Without the daily example of godly parents, children are often left to flounder.

For success in this task of spiritually training children, parents and the church must work together.

WHY PARENTS NEED THE CHURCH

Think for a moment about why parents need the church.

1. Church staff and teachers and leaders can provide backup and review to the spiritual truths the child is taught at home. They learn that other people (besides Dad and Mom) believe the Bible. Knowing Christians with a wide variety of personalities, occupations, and experiences can be significant to a questioning fifth grader or a doubting adolescent.

2. Churches can provide training in areas where a parent isn't as well qualified. For instance, my dad was also my pastor, and I would say I received 95 percent of my spiritual training from my parents.

However, I remember listening to visiting guest speakers at church who were experts on specific subjects. For instance, I remember a scientist talking to us about the flaws in the theory of evolution and another one who explained the latest biblical archaeological discoveries. Yes, my parents knew the basics of these subjects, but a doctor of biology or a biblical archaeologist could discuss details in a way my parents couldn't.

3. Churches provide a place to serve. Even very young children can collect Communion cups or hand out bulletins. Older kids can play musical instruments as an offertory or put on a skit. Teenagers can help out at Awana or in other children's ministries.

4. Churches give children an opportunity to meet other Christians. They'll get to know the little old lady who sits in the back row each Sunday, crocheting socks for servicemen. They'll get acquainted with the high school student who made the front page of the local paper because he refused to say some of the words required in the senior-class play script. Church exposes children to people of all age-groups, occupations, and personalities.

5. Churches expose children and teenagers to missionaries who have lived and served in other cultures.

6. Churches provide a social outlet for kids. What better place for kids to meet other kids than at church? (On a personal note, I know that I bypassed many temptations common to high school kids because of my church youth group. I was surrounded by friends who were taught the same biblical principles I'd been taught and who had parents, like mine, who enforced those principles.)

7. Churches teach children structure and discipline. I've had several preschool and kindergarten teachers tell me that they can usually pick out the children who attend church. Why? Because the children know how to sit still and follow directions. They've been in a classroom setting since they were babies, so they know how to listen.

At first this might not seem like a primary biblical reason for your child to attend church. But think about it: Don't we want our children to know how to listen and learn?

8. Churches have people who specifically encourage children. There's Mrs. Smith, who sends a card and a dollar bill to every child who goes to church camp; there's Pastor Brent, who has a smile and handshake for every kid who walks through the door; there's the Awana leader who shows up at the soccer games of the children he ministers to.

9. Churches provide a place for children to watch their parents serving others. They see Dad giving Communion, Mom teaching children's church, or both parents being part of the worship team or greeting people as they come in the front door of the church.

10. Churches support parents on moral principles. As children grow and have more and more questions about the rights and wrongs of life, churches can provide a place for good information and honest discussions. "What about abortion?" "What about homosexuality?" "What about sex before marriage?" "What about euthanasia?"

11. Churches can provide parenting resources through books, DVDs, and seminars.

12. Churches can establish small groups where parents can come together and discuss parenting topics.

WHY THE CHURCH NEEDS PARENTS

Then think about why the church needs the parents.

1. Biblically, parents should be the primary spiritual teachers of their children. Churches need to recognize the parents' responsibility.

2. Parents can reinforce what the children have learned at church (just as the church reinforces what the parents have taught). The consistency of the parents makes a big difference in the lives of the kids—and of the church.

3. Parents are the models children follow. If parents are saying one thing and doing another, children won't be impressed with the Christian life, no matter what they're taught at church.

4. Parents can encourage friendships between their own children and the other children in the church.

5. Parents are the people who get the children to church.

6. Parents serve in their children's classes. They open their homes to the youth or agree to go along on missions trips.

7. Parents can serve with their children in a church ministry by stocking a food bank together, singing for offertory, or e-mailing a missionary family.

8. Parents can provide resources that churches otherwise might not have. In one church, a parent who was a college-application consultant offered classes for the high school students on choosing and applying to various universities. In another church, a parent/police officer gave classes on keeping children safe on the Internet.

9. Parents can help their children understand spiritual truths one-on-one, whereas much of church teaching is done in a classroom setting.

10. Parents can help other families in the church when difficulties arise—whether that's bringing a meal to a family when someone's in the hospital or babysitting so a couple can get counseling from a church staff member.

11. Parents can spiritually "adopt" a child who comes from a broken home or has unsaved parents. This could involve anything from keeping up with how that child is doing in his memory work to inviting him along on family outings. Many adults credit their spiritual stability to the care and concern of a friend's parents.

12. Parents can lead small accountability groups and Bible studies that focus on encouraging other dads and moms.

CHAPTER 8

THE PLAN

Most churches would agree that there should be *some* kind of home-church connection in regard to the spiritual training of children, but often that connection is haphazard, misdirected, or neglected. Children's ministry is often the least important part of the overall church ministry. Sometimes this is by choice, and sometimes it's just what happens because no one's paying attention. Any correlation between the children's programs and youth programs is accidental or nonexistent.

Babies are introduced to your congregation during baby dedication, and everyone promises to pray for both parents and child. But as babies grow into toddlers, they disappear into the basement classrooms or the children's ministry wing. The congregation doesn't see them again until they graduate from high school (that is, if they're still hanging around church). Once again the kids are brought before the congregation, and everyone promises to pray for their future.

And that's it.

But that doesn't *have* to be it.

To connect with each other, the church and parents must be on the same track, and that doesn't happen by chance. You need to connect with parents more than twice in a lifetime; you need to connect with them every year—or even every month—*or every week.*

But how?

Before answering that more fully, here are some important reminders.

- You (as a church staff member or teacher or leader) will not want to do everything suggested in this book. Every church is different. But choose the suggestions that work for you, and use other suggestions as a starting point in developing a plan that *does* meet the individualized needs of your church.

- Families are different. Their schedules are different, their kids have different learning styles, and the parents have different parenting styles, even those who are equally committed to spiritually training their children. What works for one family might not work for another. (That's why, in part 1 of this book, the family itinerary plans are designed to fit each family's need.) Be cautious about implying rigid standards, such as saying, "To do this the right way, you need to have a twenty-minute time of prayer and Bible reading at the breakfast table." That just won't work for everybody. Be careful about putting all families in a nonnegotiable, structured box.

- Many families are already doing well in giving their children a solid spiritual heritage. Take advantage of their experience and expertise. Use them to lead classes or accountability groups.

GETTING STARTED

In working with parents, your goal as a church is to continually connect with them, support them, and provide them with resources and accountability as they raise their children to become modern-day Josephs—young adults who know, love, and serve God throughout their lives.

For the journey that's involved in pursuing this spiritual training, here's a complete list of age-appropriate "life threads" that parents are taught in the first part of this book:

Preschoolers: *Respect* for the awesomeness and authority of God.

Early Elementary: *Wisdom* based on the knowledge of God and His Word.

Older Elementary: Responding with *grace* in our relationships with others.

Middle School: Sensing *destiny* and purpose in doing God's will.

High School: Developing a life *perspective* based on the sovereignty of God.

Think of these as the core focus in your approach to teaching each age-group. (Read more about these "Master Life Threads" in Larry Fowler's book *Raising a Modern-Day Joseph*.)

Your Course Outline

Ages:	Master Life Thread:
Preschoolers (ages 2–5)	*Respect*
Early Elementary (ages 5–8: kindergarten to second grade)	*Wisdom*
Older Elementary (ages 8–11: third through sixth grades)	*Grace*
Middle School (ages 11–14: seventh and eighth grades)	*Destiny*
High School (ages 14–18: ninth through twelfth grades)	*Perspective*

Your Organizer

Is there someone in your church who's passionate about working with parents? Ask if he or she would be willing to be director of a church-home coordination program for spiritually training children.

This person is responsible for …

- making parents aware of the parent/church connection plan.
- planning events and launching Bible study groups and accountability groups for parents.
- connecting parents to the church and to other parents through e-mails, announcements, and phone calls.
- planning and leading the kickoff and parents' meetings (as described in the next section).
- directing the milestone celebrations (also explained in the next section).

Your Calendar

1. *Dedicate a church service to casting a vision for the importance of spiritually training children and teenagers.* The focus of the message should be twofold: (1) the importance of a family spiritually training their children, and (2) the importance of the church coming alongside the family. In a sense, this is you, the church (pastoral staff and body of believers), dedicating yourselves to helping the parents (Ephesians 4:16).

2. *Plan a kickoff meeting for parents in the fall.* This is primarily for parents who haven't previously been involved in the church/home program, though veteran parents may also attend. If you're targeting parents who don't come to church but whose children attend your Sunday school or midweek kids' program, ask a few outgoing church families to attend. They can be hosts and hostesses, helping the others to feel welcomed.

This meeting should be short (twenty minutes or so) and is for the purpose of introducing the parents to the church/parent calendar and overall program structure.

3. *Plan a parents' meeting in the fall.* Plan for approximately ninety minutes. During this meeting, reiterate the importance of the parent/church connection and include a teaching segment on one of the Master Life Threads. Discuss parenting tips and let parents know about available resources. Provide childcare so parents don't have to worry about getting a babysitter. Serve refreshments; food always provides a welcomed break.

Note: Often the best time to schedule this parents' meeting is during the time children are involved in a regular activity such as Sunday school or a midweek children's program. This is optimal timing when unchurched parents may be more apt to attend. However, don't neglect parents who are Sunday school teachers or who work as leaders in the midweek program. Schedule another parents' meeting so they (and you—if you're a parent of children or teenagers) can participate in the program.

Again, plan the meeting to fit the individualized needs of your church.

Here are some tips for a great parents' meeting.

- Begin with a welcome, prayer, and encouragement to take part in the program.
- Plan a get-acquainted activity if your church is large and parents might not know each other or there are several unchurched parents involved.
- Ask parents who have been involved in the program to share a memorable moment or a resource that has helped their family.

- Discuss a parenting topic. This could be an overview of the Master Life Threads, with an emphasis on one of the five.
- Hand out calendars with the year's events listed.
- Familiarize your parents with available resources—books in the church library, a video series on parenting, a parenting retreat, etc.
- Discuss opportunities to get involved in a parenting Bible study. (You could have the group made up of parents of a particular age-group, or you could mix the parents so dads and moms of older kids could encourage and help parents of younger kids.)
- Give the parents at least twenty minutes to work on their family itineraries. (If you encourage parents to do this at home, they probably won't get it done. That's just a fact that's true of all of us. Life gets in the way.) The family itinerary is an individualized list of family goals (see the worksheets for these at the end of each chapter in part 1.) Encourage families to include goals that will appeal to the ages of all their children, though there should be some goals that target a specific age. For instance, in a family with both a three-year-old and a twelve-year-old, making a meal for elderly neighbors could be a goal appealing to both ages. The three-year-old could make a card, and the twelve-year-old could bake the cookies.
- Make sure single parents feel welcomed. Sometimes they may need the most encouragement. Life can be overwhelming to a person doing the job of two parents and who's often holding down a full-time job at the same time. Yet they're the ones who often feel left out of a group. Put two single moms together or two single dads. (You may want to set this pairing up beforehand so they know they'll have a friend with whom to work. Otherwise, they may stay home, not wanting to feel awkward.)
- Give special encouragement to parents of teenagers. Planning a family itinerary for a household with teenagers is very different from that of a household of preschoolers. Perhaps you could have a parent/teenager meeting for your older parents so the teenagers can be part of the challenge and the planning.
- Give special encouragement to parents who don't complete their family itineraries at the meeting. Check up on them a week or two later to see if they've completed it.
- Ask the families involved in the program to come to the platform the next Sunday morning. The pastor (or church/home director) can give a brief overview of what these families are doing and then pray for wisdom for the families as they work toward their goals.

If you've been doing the family/church partnership program for a few years, ask a couple of children or parents to share what they've recently done. This could include a preschooler quoting a verse, a kindergartner singing a song, a few elementary kids acting out a Bible event, a young teenager giving a report of the service project he did with his family, a high schooler giving a short devotional, or a parent sharing a great idea that worked in his or her family.

4. *Continue to plan events throughout the year.*

- Offer parenting seminars.
- Offer Bible study groups where parents can come together, look at God's Word, and share what's been happening in their homes.
- Notify parents of any new resources in the church library or resource center.
- Plan fun family events during the year—a harvest barbecue, Christmas caroling, a winter festival, a trip to a spring ball game. The purpose of these activities is to bring the families together so parents, children, and teenagers can enjoy each other's company.

5. *Plan a milestone celebration in the spring for those families that met the goals listed on their family itineraries.*

This is a time to encourage and honor those families that are continuing with the program. You could have this milestone celebration on a night separate from other church activities or combine it with a church service or an established end-of-the-year celebration such as an Awana awards night.

Remember that children will be in a stage for more than one year. For instance, children will be learning about respect for God throughout their preschool years. Each year, the family should receive a certificate for meeting its goals.

Depending on the size of your church, you could have a milestone celebration for each age-group, or one big celebration for all ages.

As children and teenagers are ready to graduate into the next age-group, honor them in a unique and special way.

(The rest of the chapters in part 2 include special suggestions for the milestone celebration for each age-grouping.)

THE ROLE OF A MENTOR/PRAYER PARTNER

For children in the older elementary grades and up, consider assigning a mentor/prayer partner—a person or a couple—to each child in your church. (We suggest this as part of the early elementary milestone celebration.)

The primary role of someone in this position is that of an encourager. Below are some ways for this person to be involved in the child's life. (Implementing these would depend on the adult, the child, and the parents. *Nothing* should be done *without* a parent's knowledge.)

- The prayer partner can arrange a get-acquainted meeting with the parents. (Many parents and mentors will already know each other.)
- The prayer partner can send the family occasional notes reminding them he or she is praying for them.
- The prayer partner can recognize major events in the family's life—birth of a brother or sister, death of a relative, moving to a new house, winning an award, etc.
- The prayer partner can attend a child's athletic events or school programs with the parents.
- The prayer partner can encourage the child in activities such as completing his Awana handbook.
- The prayer partner can invite the child (and family) on an occasional outing. (Because of child protection standards, the adult and child should not go anywhere alone.)

The ideal would be for the mentor to encourage the family indefinitely—possibly until the child himself is an adult. But the reality in our transient society is that people often move away or change churches. So have a ready list of people willing to step in and take the place of a mentoring person or couple that is no longer in the picture.

If you don't have enough adults to serve as mentors and prayer partners, you may need to assign the participating adults to more than one family.

DOING IT TOGETHER

What else can you do in your church's ministries to children and youth to reinforce each family's Master Life Thread in their children's spiritual training? What can you do to support the parents as they raise their children and youth to be modern-day Josephs?

To answer that, you'll find plenty of ideas in the chapters to come.

CHAPTER 9

AT THE STARTING LINE
(AGES 0–2)

Don't wait until a couple has their baby. You can encourage them as soon as the expected-baby news is made public.

- Provide classes for first-time expectant parents.
- Encourage nursery staff to visit parents and welcome them to the world of the church nursery. Provide the soon-to-be parents with a list of guidelines. (This is a great outreach tool to those parents who are on the "fringes" of your church. For instance, a girl who attended your high school youth group but who no longer regularly attends church since getting married, or a woman who attends a church Bible study, or parents who have older children in your programs but don't attend church themselves.)
- Women can give baby showers with a devotional time emphasizing the importance of spiritually nurturing a child. Deuteronomy 6 would be a good choice of Scripture to highlight at this event. And don't forget unwed moms. Remember that the baby didn't choose the circumstances and that the mom could probably use a lot of love and spiritual encouragement. In larger churches, a team can be organized to make sure all new moms get showers—not just the moms whom everyone knows. Remember too that some baby showers are now for Dad *and* Mom.
- Ask expectant parents if they would like to be put on the church prayer list.

We recognize that many children are born into homes where the parenting skills of Dad and Mom are less than ideal. Sometimes this is due to lack of interest, but more often it's because of a lack of knowledge. Churches can be of particular help in these situations. But churches also need to support the more mature and self-confident parents.

AFTER THE BABY ARRIVES ...

- Visit the new parents. (Often a pastor or staff member will visit at the hospital or shortly after the baby comes home.) Always call first to make sure that the parents are comfortable with the visit, and that both Dad and Mom will be present.

- Take meals to the new parents. Many churches already do this, and church families expect it. But other families might not expect it. How about that family whose kids come to Awana? How about that single mom who lives next door to the church? Bringing meals can be an unexpected surprise and a bridge into the home.

- Provide monthly newsletters that offer tips for new parents. Many curriculums provide these, but your church could write its own, making the content specific to your church family. Use the newsletter as a way to announce upcoming parenting seminars and other events that may be of interest to new parents.

- Make sure nursery workers have had background checks and are up-to-date on your church's child protection policies. Some churches allow anyone big enough to pick up a baby to work in a nursery, but you must be careful. New parents want to know that qualified people are taking care of their children. Sometimes parents on nursery duty allow their older children to hang around the nursery area. Bad idea. What if their seven-year-old drops someone's baby? What if their middle school son breaks the rocking horse? Besides, what lesson or message is an older child missing out on by sitting in the nursery? Even if the older child *is* capable of watching a baby, new parents can feel uneasy seeing children as caretakers. You want parents to know their babies are getting the best care possible.

- Nursery workers also need to recognize that they're essential in welcoming new people. Sometimes the nursery workers are the first people whom newcomers meet. Nursery workers can be encouraging or discouraging when it comes to making guests feel at home.

Another reminder: Include families that adopt in your church new-baby traditions. Those parents also need prayer, encouragement, and meals—even parents who adopt older children.

BABY DEDICATION

Baby dedication is actually *parent* dedication. This is a time when the parents stand before the church and publicly acknowledges that they want to raise their child "in the training and instruction of the Lord" (Ephesians 6:4).

In some churches, the baby dedication is a formal ceremony with a set series of admonitions and encouragements for the parents. In other churches, the pastor might be more informal, telling of his acquaintance with the parents (especially if he's known them from childhood or performed their wedding ceremony). Other churches use a combination of both approaches.

Usually the parents are given some type of certificate to commemorate the day. This may be a certificate purchased at the local Christian bookstore, or a church can design a more personal one for each family.

The important aspect of a baby dedication is that the parents are declaring their desire to raise the child in a Christian home—and are asking the church to come alongside them by praying and encouraging that child. (Don't forget single parents who may want to dedicate their children. They also need the support and prayer of their church family.)

Here are some ideas to make the baby dedication a special event:

- If the parents feel comfortable speaking in front of groups, consider asking them to give their testimony and to tell about what they desire for their child.
- Consider asking the parents to select a verse for their child (or entire family) in recognition of their responsibility in raising their child. This can be shared with the entire congregation.

Some examples of possible verses:

> Impress them on your children. Talk about them when you sit at home and when you walk along the road, when you lie down and when you get up. (Deuteronomy 6:7)

But if serving the LORD seems undesirable to you, then choose for yourselves this day whom you will serve, whether the gods your forefathers served beyond the River, or the gods of the Amorites, in whose land you are living. But as for me and my household, we will serve the LORD. (Joshua 24:15)

Unless the LORD builds the house, its builders labor in vain. Unless the LORD watches over the city, the watchmen stand guard in vain.… Sons are a heritage from the LORD, children a reward from him. Like arrows in the hands of a warrior are sons born in one's youth. Blessed is the man whose quiver is full of them. They will not be put to shame when they contend with their enemies in the gate. (Psalm 127:1, 3–5)

Train a child in the way he should go, and when he is old he will not turn from it. (Proverbs 22:6)

Then little children were brought to Jesus for him to place his hands on them and pray for them. But the disciples rebuked those who brought them. Jesus said, "Let the little children come to me, and do not hinder them, for the kingdom of heaven belongs to such as these." (Matthew 19:13–14)

- In some churches, the parents or the pastor or children's ministry director writes a letter to the child being dedicated, and the letter is to be sealed and left unopened until the child's eighteenth birthday. This letter states the purpose of the dedication, the seriousness of the responsibility that the parents and church feel toward the child, and their shared desire for the child to become an adult reflecting the qualities Joseph possessed in his own life.
- The pastor or staff member letter can speak about the parents' desire to see their child trusting the Lord Jesus Christ as personal Savior and then walking with Christ daily throughout life.

CHAPTER 10

PRESCHOOLERS (AGES 2–5)

MASTER LIFE THREAD: RESPECT (GENESIS 39:6–9)

MORE SUGGESTIONS FOR CHURCHES HELPING FAMILIES

1. *Use every opportunity to teach preschoolers.* Too many churches think of preschool ministry as babysitting, or they don't offer classes for children until they're school age. Preschoolers are at an impressionable age. They're more willing to accept what they're taught than at any other time in their lives. We should ask God for wisdom in guiding these developing minds.

2. *Train children's workers to emphasize the importance of respecting the awesomeness of God.* Too often we tell "Bible stories" with the focus on the person rather than on God. Yes, Daniel was brave and prayed to God even when told not to. And, yes, Daniel was thrown into the lions' den (not pleasant overnight accommodations). But God's power is what closed those lions' mouths—not the courage of Daniel. We need to put the emphasis on our heavenly Father.

3. *Encourage men to get involved in preschool children's ministry.* Not only does this help single moms have a male influence in their children's lives, but it also shows young children that church is for women *and* men.

4. *Make your church a safe place for children.* Require your workers to go through background checks and your child protection course. Let parents know you have these requirements so they feel secure entrusting their children to your care.

5. *Be intentional about telling children that God loves them and that people in the church (including you) love them too.* You want to create a sense of belonging to the people and the place. Too many children today (even preschoolers) have everything, including piles of toys (and even shelves full of trophies), signifying how special they are. What else do they need? Their perception *can be* that they don't need the church or the teachers or God. We have a responsibility to show them their need.

I remember a mom calling Awana because she was upset that our curriculum stated everyone had sinned. She claimed her daughter hadn't sinned, so our curriculum offended her daughter. We had to tell the mom that the Bible clearly states that everyone has sinned and that everyone was born a sinner. (Wouldn't you like to meet that perfect third grader?)

6. *Be intentional about room planning.* Churches must create a warm, friendly, second-home atmosphere for children. We need to establish a place of security and trust—only then will they listen to what we have to say. Are your classrooms colorful, appealing, and safe? Does cheerful music welcome the kids? Are there pictures on the walls that the children have colored, glued, cut, and flooded with glitter? Make your classrooms inviting.

7. *Be enthusiastic.* Welcome the child (and parents) to church. Convey a good attitude, and communicate that something exciting is happening. Teachers should arrive *before* the children. Lights should be on and music playing. This is *the* place to be! (Sadly, in too many churches, children show up to still dark and empty classrooms because the teachers are across town, stuck in a drive-through lane waiting for their lattes.)

8. *Show respect to God during prayer time by encouraging quietness.* Many children continue playing, coloring, or chatting when someone's praying. One way for children to be taught reverence is for adults to be reverent. Too often adults congregate in the back of the room and chat, even though the lead teacher is praying with the children.

Teach preschoolers to fold their hands and close their eyes—and then remind them that the reason we do so is to focus on what we're doing. (If our eyes are closed, we won't look around. If our hands are folded, we won't poke the friend next to us.) But children also need to know that they can pray anywhere in any position. God hears us wherever we are and whatever we're doing—even when our eyes are open.

9. *Make sure all teachers explain the gospel in similar terms.* We notice that some children respond to every invitation to trust Christ, even when they've done it just the week before. Teachers unknowingly can be part of the problem. Over the period of several weeks, the child might hear the following:

- If you want to go to heaven, talk to one of the teachers.
- If you want to ask Jesus into your heart, raise your hand.
- If you want Jesus to be your friend, come talk to me.
- If you want to trust Christ as Savior, talk to Pastor Dan after class.

We may think a child is confused about what he's done—but often adults are the ones confusing the child. Terms need to be consistent.

10. *Communicate with parents so they know the terms you use when explaining salvation to children.* That way teachers and parents are consistent in their terminology, which eliminates confusion.

11. *Use the Bible (even though many young children can't read).* Show the children the Bible as you teach. Remind them that the Bible is God's message to us. Read at least one verse from the Bible during the lesson. In many churches, people no longer bring their Bibles because the Scripture is put on an overhead screen or in a bulletin. Preschoolers need to see the actual book. Be intentional about pointing out the location of the verse or Bible event in Scripture.

When I taught preschool Sunday school, some of the children would bring their own Bibles to class. I would choose one of their Bibles and teach the lesson from that child's Bible instead of my own. This was fun for the children, and they often begged me to use their Bible. By doing this, I was making them feel important while subtly teaching them that all Bibles are the same, even though they might look different. Besides, their Bibles often had a lot more colorful pictures than mine!

12. *Make sure children know the difference between which stories are fiction and which biographies (stories) come from the Bible.* Often in preschool ministry we have funny puppets doing funny things, then go right into the Bible lesson, not realizing that in the very literal mind of a three- or four-year-old, it's all the same.

An easy way to teach the difference is to change location. When you're telling a fictional story or watching a puppet show, have the children sit on the floor. When you're teaching from the Bible, have the children sit on chairs. (Or do the opposite.) You can teach children that when they see the Bible in the teacher's hands they're hearing true words from God.

PRESCHOOL MILESTONE CELEBRATION

The preschool milestone celebration is a time to honor those families that have reached their family itinerary goals. Remember, you'll have families that are celebrating their first year in the preschool age-group and some families whose children will soon be graduating into early elementary.

Preschoolers love lots of color, balloons, and age-appropriate excitement. You could do this through decorations, music, etc. If you have a small group, give each family opportunity to share what they have learned. This could include quoting family verses, singing a song, or telling of a special activity done to reinforce the goals. If you have a large group, choose three or four to participate. (Do this beforehand so they can prepare.)

Each family that has reached their family itinerary goals should receive a certificate of completion.

Give an award such as a children's Bible to those preschoolers graduating into early elementary. Put the child's name, date, and church on the inside front cover. The pastor or teacher could write a personal note to each child to make the gift unique. Award the Bibles with a lot of applause and picture taking. Ask the children (and their parents) to stand on the platform with their Bibles while the pastor prays for them.

Give the parents a copy of their child's picture, and encourage them to start a scrapbook detailing their child's spiritual journey.

Another celebration option: Choose a unique setting—reserve a site at a park, or have a bonfire in someone's backyard. Talk about how God's creation is evident all around. He has done so much for us; we need to respect Him in return. Children this age love being outdoors, and such a celebration would be truly memorable.

CHAPTER 11

EARLY ELEMENTARY
(AGES 5–8: KINDERGARTEN THROUGH SECOND GRADE)

MASTER LIFE THREAD: WISDOM (GENESIS 40:6–8)

MORE SUGGESTIONS FOR CHURCHES HELPING FAMILIES

1. *Start a parent blog.* Blogs are easy to set up, yet difficult to keep up. But blogs kept up to date can be a great church/parent communication tool. They can update parents on church events, upcoming themes, reminders to get their child's permission slip in, and outlines of lessons. Blogs can also be used to list resources or let parents know of an upcoming special event at church.

Some blog rules:

Be consistent. If you'd rather do a weekly post rather than daily, that's fine, but let people know that you'll post on a particular day each week—and then do it.

Be brief. Keep to the point.

Be legal. Since you're writing about a Sunday school class, Awana club, or other children's ministry, the tendency is to post cute pictures of all the cute kids in your church. Don't do it without a signed permission form from the parents. This is of major importance and something that many churches neglect. (Hand out permission forms at the beginning of the year as part of the registration process.)

Be sensitive. Don't write posts like this: "We had a great night, except for Danny M., who wouldn't listen." Or, "Please pray for the parents of one of our first graders; they're going through a messy divorce." Obviously parents will figure out who you're talking about.

2. *Communicate with parents when you see the child take an interest in trusting Christ.* If you notice that a child is asking questions about salvation and you can sense a decision is about to be made, talk to the parents. Tell them what you've observed and that you'll be praying for them as they talk to their child. This gives the parents the opportunity to have the privilege of leading their child to Christ. If a child does trust Christ at church, the teacher/leader should immediately tell the parents. If the parents are unsaved, invite them to sit in as you talk to the child about salvation.

3. *Learn the names of the children in your group.* We all like to feel important. When someone doesn't remember our name or misspells it, we feel unimportant. Even as adults we feel rather offended when someone calls us the wrong name, though we understand some people have bad memories.

Children, too, like to feel noticed. When you say "John" and the boy's name is "Jared," he notices. Or if you refer to him as "one of the Johnson boys," he notices that too. He doesn't want to be confused with his brothers. He wants to be noticed for being *him.*

If you're bad with names, ask the children to wear nametags until you get it right.

4. *Invite parents to share activities they've done at home* to teach about a particular Bible character or facts they've discovered while doing research. (Interesting research findings can be put on the parent blog.) If a family wrote a play about a Bible character, ask the family to perform it for a children's class at church.

5. *Understand that early elementary–age children respond well to repetition.* Sometimes the best teaching method is reviewing, again and again.

For instance, I wanted to teach a group of children in this age-group the books of the Bible. To start each week's meeting, we would say them together. At the beginning of the year, teachers were the only ones participating. By the end of the year, we didn't have to say anything. The children could repeat all the books with confidence. What do you want to teach? Review it once a week, and eventually most of the children will be able to say it themselves.

6. *Choose one Bible character's life or one major event to reenact.* Ask parents to help with costuming, staging, and script. If you have some talented songwriters in your church, they could write music to go along with your reenactment. Invite parents, friends, and other church people to watch the skit. Check out Christian theaters for productions of plays focusing on a Bible character or event.

7. *Ask pastors and other staff members to talk to your class about their favorite Bible character.* Ask the guest speakers to tell the children why they chose that character, what that character did, and how the character obeyed (or disobeyed) God.

8. *Give children an opportunity to pray.* You could encourage this by giving them something specific to pray for: "I would like each one of you to thank God for something or someone in your life."

9. *Teach children that prayer is a time when we should be quiet and respectful to God.* Teach boys to remove their hats. Teach all children to sit (or stand) quietly with eyes closed, hands folded, and heads bowed. Explain that we do that to keep from being distracted.

Adults, too, should be quiet and respectful in prayer time, which means they shouldn't be clustered in the back of the room, adding up points, sharing cake recipes, or drinking coffee.

At the same time, you need to teach children that they can pray anywhere. They don't have to wait until they're sitting quietly. They can pray on the school bus, at the park or the ball game, etc.

10. *Choose children who can read to look up Scripture for your lesson.* Write the reference on an index card, and hand it to the child before the lesson. Tell the child to find the verse and bookmark the page with the card. When you reach the point in the lesson when you'll be talking about that verse, call on the child to read it. You might want to assign a teacher to listen to the child read the verse (before class begins) so the teacher can have help with any unfamiliar words.

11. *Assign children to bring something to class that you can use as a visual example in the lesson.* (You could give a small treat to children who do so.)

Some examples:

Creation—Children bring in something God created.

Noah's ark—Children bring stuffed animals.

Joshua and the battle of Jericho—Children bring an instrument. Explain that the army carried trumpets made of rams' horns. Show them a picture of a ram's horn.

The Lord Jesus is the Light of the World—Children bring a type of light.

12. *For those children graduating out of early elementary, assign a prayer partner to each child and his or her family.* (See the discussion of this in chapter 8.) The role of this person or couple is to mentor and encourage. This could look different, depending on the family with whom they're matched. Some may offer only prayer support. Others may be more involved in the child's life, actually helping the child to learn about the Bible or to memorize verses.

Don't forget your church's single parents. Assign a couple to act as prayer partners to the children of single moms. Choose older, grandparent-type people who can provide encouragement and a male role model. Do the same with a single dad, assigning an older couple in which the woman could become a true friend to any girls in the family.

EARLY ELEMENTARY MILESTONE CELEBRATION

The early elementary milestone celebration is a time to honor those families that have reached their family itinerary goals. Remember, you'll have families that are celebrating their first year in the early elementary age-group and some families whose children will soon be graduating into older elementary.

Make the evening special. You could do this through decorations, music, etc. Give several families opportunity to share what they've learned. (This could be quoting family verses, singing a song, or telling of a special activity done to reinforce the goal.) The evening could be combined with an Awana awards night.

Each family should receive a certificate of completion. Assign a mentor/prayer partner to those children moving on to older elementary classes. (See above.)

Another option—choose a children's speaker to be part of the celebration. Choose someone (or a group) who will talk about a Bible character in a unique way. This could be through a puppet show, ventriloquism, or storytelling. Make sure the person is committed to giving an accurate presentation. You don't want to undo what you've spent the year teaching. (When thinking about whom to invite, don't overlook your own teachers or someone else in your church. Sometimes they're the best "guest" speakers. They know what the children have learned, and they know your goals for the groups. Perhaps a teacher could dress up as David, Joshua, or Paul and give a monologue of the Bible character's life.)

CHAPTER 12

OLDER ELEMENTARY
(AGES 8–11: THIRD THROUGH SIXTH GRADES)

MASTER LIFE THREAD: GRACE (GENESIS 41:51–52)

MORE SUGGESTIONS FOR CHURCHES HELPING FAMILIES

1. *Plan a special get-together* for the children, their families, and their mentor/prayer partners, giving them a time to strengthen friendships.

2. *Be alert to children who attend your church without their parents.* (This happens more often beginning at this age.) Invite the parents to attend. Assign a couple to be that child's mentor/prayer partner, but the connection should take place only inside the church with other people around. Perhaps the couple listens to the child recite her verses in Awana or meets with the child for a few minutes before church to see how he's doing. Don't encourage mentor/prayer partners to connect with the child outside of church unless the child's parents initiate it and are present.

3. *Give children opportunities to show grace to one another.* Plan a series of lessons on how to show God's grace to those around us:

- In the home with parents, brothers, sisters.

- With friends.
- At church, even when you're teamed with someone who's unlikable or doesn't do well.
- When everything goes wrong and you're angry at the world.
- When someone's facing a tough situation.

4. *Introduce the children to the people who lead your church.* Ask people from different church ministries to explain what they do. (This could be a Sunday school lesson, Awana large-group lesson, or part of your other children's ministries.)

Invite church ministry leaders and staff to talk to the kids about their service responsibilities. This could include pastors, elders, deacons, trustees, worship team members, missions team members, children's ministry team members, women's Bible study teacher, etc.

5. *Introduce the children to your church's doctrinal statement.* You don't need to spend hours on each point, but briefly explain (in age-appropriate language) what they mean. Invite the parents to the classes so they hear what you're saying and can answer questions their children may have. (Actually some parents probably don't know what your church believes, and this will be a teaching time for them too.) Children this age like to feel grown up, so honor them by telling them that they're a part of the church and that's why they need to know what the church believes.

6. *Explain church ordinances to the children.* Tell them the whys and hows of the Lord's Supper (Communion) and water baptism. Make sure they understand what these ordinances mean and what they should know before taking part. Again, invite parents to be part of this. They need to know what you're saying to their children.

7. *Invite the church treasurer or financial secretary to talk with the children.* Younger children may think money goes straight from the offering plate to God. (We tell them they're giving to God, so their conclusion makes sense.) Other kids think the money goes straight to the pastor. Ask the treasurer or financial secretary to tell the children the different ways the church uses the money: upkeep, missions, salaries, paper and other supplies, curriculum, electricity, heat, snowplowing, etc. You could also explain that churches have safeguards in counting the money and getting it to the bank. (The pastor doesn't count it and keep it at his house.)

Children need to understand they save money by not wasting paper or by making sure lights are turned off in empty classrooms.

8. *Organize a team of kids to write a brochure about the children's ministries in your church.* Encourage

them to take pictures of different classrooms and events. Assign a team to design the brochure on the computer. Print the brochure and distribute it to families in your neighborhood or to new families (with children) that attend the church. Praise the children for their hard work, and pray with them that God would use the brochure to reach other kids.

9. *Teach a series of lessons on apologetics to your fifth and sixth graders.* At this age, you don't want to give them information overload. Focus on a few facts. For example, you could focus on the discovery of the Hittite civilization, the findings of the Dead Sea Scrolls, or the fulfillment of Isaiah 9:6.

10. *Plan children's events at church missions conferences.* Children need to know that people serve the Lord in different capacities. Purposely choose missionaries who can relate to children and youth. Missionaries could …

- serve a traditional meal from the country where they serve.
- teach a game from their country.
- teach a verse or song in the language.
- talk about unusual customs in the country.
- show a DVD about the country.
- share how and why they became a missionary.

Children need to sense the joy of not only knowing and loving God but also of serving Him. The calling of many missionaries began in response to a missionary they met or a message they heard from a missionary while in the third-to-sixth-grade years.

11. *Plan missions trips for entire families.* These don't have to be to some exotic place across an ocean. You can serve an inner-city mission or a paint a cabin at a camp for underprivileged children.

12. *Recognize that not every lesson needs an application.* Some lessons need to be taught simply to aid a child's understanding of Scripture and to encourage a loving response to our magnificent, awesome, glorious heavenly Father—and not to go out and *do* something. The current trend in children's ministry curriculum is to tack on applications to everything. They don't always make sense, and they take the focus off the main point and put it on a superficial application. Applications are good, but they aren't always necessary.

I like what Cheryl Dunlop writes in her book *Follow Me as I Follow Christ:*

[T]he danger of applying every lesson by encouraging student action is that a child may subtly pick up something we do not intend to teach: that Christianity is defined by something we do. It was exactly this misperception that Paul was attacking when he said, "Are you so foolish? Having begun in the Spirit, are you now being made perfect by the flesh?" (Galatians 3:3 NKJV). (Chicago: Moody, 2000, p. 123)

13. *Plan a talent show where third to sixth graders can show off their skills.* You might be surprised! Many children this age take band or orchestra at school, draw, do illusions, or sing. Tell them that their talent has to portray one thing they've learned about the Bible during the year.

OLDER ELEMENTARY MILESTONE CELEBRATION

The older elementary milestone celebration is a time to honor those families that have reached their family itinerary goals. Present certificates to all families of third-to-sixth graders that have reached their goals.

Make it a special celebration for those graduating into middle school.

Choose a service assignment for those older elementary kids who are graduating into middle school. The assignment should be chosen with the parents' consent. The purpose of the responsibility is to recognize the child as being part of the church, to teach the child about responsibility and service, and to give the child opportunity to show grace to others.

Before handing out the job assignments, challenge the children. Emphasize that having a responsibility is a privilege and that they need to do their jobs consistently and responsibly.

Possible job assignments:

- For musicians—play the offertory once a quarter.
- For artists—be part of the team designing posters for the missions conference or vacation Bible school.
- For budding writers—be part of the team working on a children's ministry brochure.
- For those who enjoy the outdoors—spend two hours a month helping the landscaping person or crew to clean up the churchyard.

- For those who enjoy working with younger children—help out in the nursery or another classroom of much younger children once a quarter.
- For those who are good workers—spend two hours a month helping the maintenance crew clean the church.
- For those interested in missions—assign them to a missionary's kid of a similar age. Their job is to e-mail and keep in contact.

Emphasize the importance of the assignments. You want the kids to understand this isn't busy work, but a responsibility that make them an integral part of the church.

Another celebration option: You could invite a kid-friendly, biblical archaeologist to give a presentation, or invite a person from a Jewish mission to demonstrate a Passover meal, or watch a DVD about a missionary.

CHAPTER 13

MIDDLE SCHOOL
(AGES 11–14: SEVENTH AND EIGHTH GRADES)

MASTER LIFE THREAD: DESTINY (GENESIS 45:4–10)

MORE SUGGESTIONS FOR CHURCHES HELPING FAMILIES

1. *Encourage families to get together throughout the year to participate in activities with their teenagers.* Plan some church family activities for everyone. Make sure single parents know they're welcome. Invite singles (those without families) to help in the planning and organization so they, too, feel part of the church family.

2. *Make your church middle school friendly.* We talk a lot about making a church kid friendly, but churches also need to be middle school friendly. Are your teenagers continuing in their responsibilities (given at the end of sixth grade)? Do they know the pastor? (Or if it's a large church, the middle school pastor?) Does the pastor use the good things the middle schoolers have done as sermon illustrations? Are they encouraged to take part in church outreach? (They can pass out brochures in the neighborhood as well as an adult can.)

This is the age so many kids drop out of church. Make your teenagers feel wanted and needed and a valuable part of your church community.

3. Choose your teachers and ministry leaders wisely. This is true with any age-group, but middle schoolers especially need adults in their lives who will teach God's Word in a gentle manner—not preaching or judging, but relating to, respecting, and encouraging the teenagers.

An example of a teacher who didn't do that: A family visited a church for the first time. Their middle school daughter wore shoes that were stylish, but made her wobble and trip across the floor. The teacher laughed and said, "You look ridiculous!" Although the family continued attending the church, the girl never made friends or related to anyone there. She'd been offended, and she didn't forget it. As soon as she was old enough, she left the church.

4. Since middle school students are questioning a lot of life choices, *develop a resource library for parents that help them in teaching a biblical response to abortion, homosexuality, racism, premarital sex, drugs, alcohol, etc.* Sometimes parents who desire to teach their kids about difficult subjects don't know how to do it or have so little knowledge about the subject that they hesitate. Come alongside them and provide the tools they need.

5. Offer a purity seminar for middle schoolers. Make it optional (not during a regular Sunday school class or youth meeting) for those families that would prefer to do this teaching at home. (A thought: Even if parents do teach purity in the home, having their teenagers attend the class will support what they've taught. Teenagers will also recognize that they're in this together—with their friends. Remember, peer pressure isn't always bad.)

6. Choose a Bible character, and make a DVD of the person's life. You can make it as professional or amateurish as you like. Choose a Bible character who had a sense of destiny in doing God's will.

I worked with a group of middle schoolers on a production of Esther. We used an old velvet drape for Esther's robe and a plastic riding toy from the nursery as the horse. Our work resulted in a presentation that we showed to both the younger classes and the adults. The girls learned about Esther in a way that they still remember many years later.

7. Encourage teamwork among middle schoolers. Instead of asking one young teenager to set up the Sunday school room, ask two or three. Instead of having an individual Bible memory contest, divide the teenagers into teams. Stay away from games where the focus is on an individual teenager. Teenagers don't like to be the center of attention, and if they fail or are in any way embarrassed by what happens, they'll not forget their humiliation.

8. Make sure the church library has books and DVDs for this age-group. Often church libraries focus on books for younger children and adults and forget youth. Supply books about creation/evolution, devotionals, fiction, missionary biographies, etc. Then let the teenagers know they're available.

9. *Involve your middle schoolers in a mission project.* They need to meet ordinary people doing extraordinary service for the Lord. Focus on one or two missionaries who occasionally visit the church (so the teenagers can get to know them). Choose tangible mission projects such as saving money for a missionary to get a new computer or saving money for twenty-five Bibles to be given to an organization that works in a third-world country.

10. *Plan a middle school Sunday.* Allow your middle schoolers to do as much of the service as possible. They can pass out bulletins, take up the offering, choose songs, play guitar or piano, lead the music, read the Scripture, and lead in prayer. Did you do a media production on the life of a Bible character? Show that to the congregation. Think of all the ways the kids can take part in the service.

11. *Write letters or send e-mails to your teenagers.* The pastor or youth pastor can write a letter to each middle schooler, letting her know how much she's appreciated as part of the church family. Make each letter different (because they *will* compare). Mention specific circumstances: "Thanks for helping out with the nursery during kids' club. You did a good job." "Thanks for helping Mr. Smith rake the leaves. You were a big help." "Thanks for having a great smile. You light up the church when you walk in."

12. *Appreciate them.* When a group of kids was surveyed as to how they thought the adults perceived them, they answered, "They don't like us." I had a young teenager tell me: "They can't find a Sunday school teacher for our class because adults are afraid of us."

How sad. Sure, they can behave strangely when they're together in a group. But when you get to know them one-on-one, that strangeness disappears. You see them as individual creations of God who are fun to be with. They're bubbling over with ideas and thoughts and love for the Lord. And they can be surprisingly sensitive.

When my husband unexpectedly passed away a few years ago, it was the middle school girls who greeted me with big hugs *every time* I walked in the church door. They would ask me, "How are you doing?" and if I answered "Fine," they would say, "No, how are you really doing?" (They *still* greet me with a hug every time they see me.) Meanwhile some of the adults avoided me; although they cared, they didn't know what to say.

Change the perception of middle schoolers in your church. Get to know them by name. Ask how they're doing. What are their interests? You might be surprised at the maturity some of them possess.

MIDDLE SCHOOL MILESTONE CELEBRATION

The middle school milestone celebration needs to be different from that of the younger children. Even if you have the preschool and elementary celebrations at one event, you may want to separate the middle school and high school celebrations to another time.

If you honor all ages at one time at a Sunday service, a spring program, or an Awana awards night, separate the younger kids from the older kids with some music or another program segment.

The middle school milestone celebration is a time to honor those families that have reached their family itinerary goals.

Some suggestions for a middle school milestone celebration:

- Give certificates to those families that have completed their goals.
- Arrange age-appropriate music.
- Challenge the teenagers with a short message about the importance of yielding to God's will and trusting Him to orchestrate their destiny.
- Challenge the teenagers to stay pure by avoiding temptation and having the courage to say no when their friends are encouraging them to do the wrong thing. The senior pastor or youth pastor could give this challenge because he would be familiar with what the teenagers have studied during the year. If you do ask a special guest to speak, make sure he knows the goals of the celebration.
- Give the teenagers opportunity to commit themselves to doing God's will in the future. (The future includes the next minute and every minute after that.)

Divide into family groups. (Again, be conscious of single parents.) Parents meet with their own daughter or son. Ask parents and teenagers to pray together about the teenager's future. Explain that making this commitment doesn't mean the teenager will be a pastor, missionary, or church musician; he's simply dedicating himself to doing what God wants him to do.

The pastor and others in church leadership could quietly walk around the room, answer any questions, or encourage discussions in families where there seems to be a lack of communication.

Tell families of graduating middle schoolers that there'll be a public dedication service at church on Sunday. Teenagers who want to be involved need to seek out the pastor (or whoever is in charge) on their own. (Requiring teenagers to initiate their willingness to participate will eliminate those who aren't serious or who are doing it because "all my friends did it.")

Another celebration option: Middle schoolers don't attend fancy dinners all that often, so why not plan one? The uniqueness of the occasion can help them remember the seriousness of what they hear from the pastor (or youth pastor or home/church director) and what they promise to the Lord.

CHAPTER 14

HIGH SCHOOL
(AGES 14–18: NINTH THROUGH TWELFTH GRADES)

MASTER LIFE THREAD: PERSPECTIVE (GENESIS 50:15–21)

MORE SUGGESTIONS FOR CHURCHES HELPING FAMILIES

1. *Allow teenagers to have major responsibilities in the church.* They could be part of the music team, usher, teach a class of young children, or even preach a sermon in the pastor's absence. (Many pastors remember their first sermon taking place when they were teenagers filling in for their own pastor.)

2. *Have an ongoing teenager journal at your church (kept in a safe place).* Ask your seniors to write in the journal and include the following:

- Name
- Future plans (college, career, military)
- Verse that means a lot to them and why
- A memory of growing up in the church

Use the same book year after year as a continuing record of the young people who consider your church their home church.

3. *Put your teenagers to work.* They can clean, plan music, decorate for the missions banquet, plant flowers, paint a room (you might want supervision here), write e-mails to missionaries, do dramas, etc.

4. *Assign your teenagers and their parents to team-teach a vacation Bible school class or children's church.*

5. *Ask the parents to write down their experiences.* When you hear about a family that has done a fun and meaningful family project, ask them to describe what they did and send it to you electronically. Keep an online book of the different ideas. Not only is this a journal of what families in your church have done, but it can encourage new parents and provide a resource to those who do the family itineraries.

Teenagers could organize the journal into a scrapbook or a Web site detailing the different family experiences.

6. *Assign someone on the pastoral staff to talk with the teenagers individually.* Ask about their future. Where will they attend college? What are their plans? Let them know the church is interested and will be praying for them as they begin a new chapter of life.

7. *Put your teenagers on your church welcoming committee.* Nothing impresses a church visitor more than having a teenager welcome him! Seriously, I've seen it happen, and it works. Assign them to serve at your information desk and to watch for new people. A responsible teenager can tell a visitor where to find a particular classroom or how to sign up for the parenting seminar as well as an adult.

8. *Gather together the teenagers who are interested in drama and have them write and produce a drama about biblical perspective.* Ask them to present the drama during a service.

9. *Ask different families to participate in nursing home or rescue mission services.* Often churches are involved one night a month. Teenagers can work with their dads and moms in presenting music, drama, or a devotional (perhaps with an object lesson).

10. *Take advantage of get-acquainted weekends at Bible colleges where they introduce prospective freshmen to the classes, the campus, and college life in general.* Visit the colleges as a group. Even kids who already know their future plans can enjoy these trips. Talk to professors. Talk to students who attend the college.

11. *Get the teenagers a couple of video cameras and have them make a DVD of the year.* Tell them to include the teenagers singing, sharing favorite verses, and discussing what they learned from their Bible

study. Include footage of them playing games or goofing off. At the end of the year, have someone edit it and put it on a DVD. Make copies for all the teenagers.

HIGH SCHOOL MILESTONE CELEBRATION—PERSPECTIVE

You may want to hold the high school milestone celebration during a regular church service, recognizing that this is a culmination of so many years of growth and hard work.

Award certificates to families that have completed their family itineraries. And honor high school graduates in an extra-special way, such as these:

- Give a short bio of each teenager, highlighting his or her honors, interests, and future plans.
- Choose music that correlates with what the teenagers have accomplished. Or ask the teenagers to each choose a song for the program. Are any of the teenagers musical? Ask them to sing or play their instrument. Is one of them a good teacher? Ask her to give a short devotional. An artist could design the program covers. A technical whiz could run the sound system. Let them shine. Let them know you're proud of their accomplishments.
- Give them a study Bible with their name engraved on the front. Ask the pastor or youth pastor (or both) to write an inscription inside the front cover (or you could give them a Bible software program).
- Challenge the congregation (as in a baby dedication) to pray for and encourage these teenagers as they go off to college or start a career. They still need connection. They still need the support of their family and church.

AND BEYOND

When students graduate from high school and move on, is there anything else churches can do for them?

Here are some suggestions:

- *Pray.* (Mentor/prayer partners can still be involved in their lives.)
- Send care packages.
- Provide a college/career Sunday school class or Bible study.
- Send bulletins or church newsletters.
- Communicate through e-mail, snail mail, or phone, giving encouraging messages to the students. (Some pastors regularly write to college students or those in the military.) Get a page on a social network—one that your college students are on—for quick and easy communication. Do a daily newsy/devotional blog they can access.
- Provide a place where students can share what they're learning in college—good or bad. The pastor of one church taught the college-age class during the summer months. He willingly gave the students a forum to discuss troubling statements they heard from professors or read in a textbook. Because of the openness of the class and his willingness to listen, he was able to defuse several erroneous ideas.
- Visit them on their college campuses or military bases. They'll appreciate their pastor, youth pastor, or anyone from their home church stopping by. Visitors can gain even more favor by taking them out to lunch. (Most college students usually are both hungry and poor.)

Most of all, be thankful to the Lord for young adults who have grown up to know, love, and serve Him—and pray that they'll go on to a lifetime of imparting those same qualities to future generations.